D0707862

This book is to be returned on or before
the last date stamped below.

Some contemporary poets of Britain and Ireland

# Some contemporary poets of Britain and Ireland

*an anthology*

edited by MICHAEL SCHMIDT

*Carcanet Press, Manchester*

First published in 1983 by
CARCANET PRESS LIMITED
in association with *PN Review*
208-212 Corn Exchange Buildings
Manchester M4 3BQ

ISBN 0 85635 469 4


*Carcanet acknowledges the financial assistance of the Arts Council of Great Britain.*

*Printed in England by SRP Ltd., Exeter*

# CONTENTS

I wish to thank those publishers who understood clearly the predicament of the contemporary anthologist and by their understanding made this book possible, in particular Tom Fenton of Salamander Press Edinburgh, Peter Jay of Anvil Press Poetry, and Neil Astley of Bloodaxe Books. I regret that I was unable to include work by Craig Raine. I had intended to print eight of his poems here.

This anthology was originally projected as a sequel to my *Eleven British Poets* (Methuen, 1980) and was to include individual introductions and notes to the work of each poet. On reflection I decided to dispense with all but the barest biographical and bibliographical indications, in the belief that good poems can pull their weight without a team of footnotes, and that good readers do not require direction.

M.S.

# PREFACE

ANTHOLOGIES of contemporary poetry often flatter their readers with promises of radical novelty, new beginnings, even 'decisive shifts of sensibility'. Yet what strikes me most about the work of my contemporaries is how readily it accommodates itself within the English traditions. At times a distantly Victorian spirit seems to be ghosting our literary world at this far end of our century. The age is Elizabethan only by accident.

The great Anglo-American modernists—who seemed so decisively to have shaken off the nineteenth century—have not been, and now perhaps never will be, assimilated into the 'mainstream' of British writing (even though Eliot and Pound, as most teachers know, remain more challenging and 'contemporary' to young readers than any of their successors). It is an academic foolishness to describe the younger 'mainstream' poets as being 'post-modernist' in anything but chronological terms. Of course they have picked up useful skills, at first or second hand, from the modernists, but very few of them have passed that way in anything like a spirit of receptive apprenticeship.

There are several conditions, coincidences and echoes which recall the preparatory disorientation of the late nineteenth century. There is a rather large market for verse, though now based primarily on the academy; journalists are interested in the poet and the poetry business, if not in the poem. The 'product' is personalized. Many of the younger writers are from the great Victorian cities and studied at provincial universities: they have lived among ruins rather than monuments, and the sense of social privilege does not attach to them. In some cases, social privilege is the last phrase that would suggest itself. Yet there are other forms of privilege: all are to one degree or another *poetae docti*, and twelve of them at least occupy or have occupied academic posts.

In some of these writers there is an Arnoldian earnestness: committed, secular, at odds with the age and its intractable forces and puzzled at their place in it. What can the poem *do*? What is its use? What does the poet count for? 'To the Linen Hall' by Tom Paulin is an eloquent *ars poetica*. It evokes an eighteenth-century library that symbolizes the Enlightenment, at the heart of a city torn by modern strife, Belfast. But it is characteristic in its pared-down manner and in its desire to speak for, as well as to speak; to be responsible and to be seen to be so in a very specific, civic sense. Read in conjunction with his poem 'The Garden of Self-delight', it points up the paradox at the heart of much of the work here: a political paradox, differently developed in Jeffrey Wainwright's 'Thomas Müntzer' and in Tony Harrison's poems, where the terms are no longer self-consciously *cultural* (poems about the place of poems) but more directly political. Harrison and Wainwright, the one writing 'from the life' and the other obliquely, out of history, address their wider subjects in a way hardly open to Paulin, with the cultural antecedents which complicate each of his utterances. Their themes are similar: the distance between aspiration and reality, or between the historical nature of the 'State' and ideas of 'Justice', terms taken up in the title of Paulin's first book and suggested in the ambiguous title of Wainwright's collection *Heart's Desire*.

Ruskin has touched other poets here—Clive Wilmer in particular. And readers may justifiably sense the presence of Thomas Hardy, A. E. Housman and Edward Thomas. The roots of these younger poets go much deeper than the nineteenth century, of course, and most of them are closely familiar with non-English writing, but all of them have some affinities with the literature and the civic and moral conflicts of that time, and in some instances the terms and forms they use are developed from those that were current then.

Most of the work collected in *Some Contemporary Poets of Britain and Ireland* is from the last decade or so, the decade since the death of W. H. Auden; and yet the voice of the tart and mannered middle-to-late Auden is audible here, too, dictating in some cases a social tone and in others setting technical challenges. It is hard not to hear him in the often very humorous work of Peter Scupham and James Fenton, for instance. Their differences in theme, technique and tone have much to do with the fecundity of Auden's example. He remains a presiding spirit. Readers may be surprised to find how little the poets of the previous generation—Hughes and Larkin in particular—impinge on this one. There is only limited communication between the visceral 1960s, the ironic 1950s, and the best writers who have emerged in the last decade or so. Thom Gunn still casts a spell, but he has been taken up as a strict and suggestive formal exemplar only by a few, and they do not write to sound like him.

It is worth noting how prolific some of the poets are. Tony Harrison's apparently endless sequence of Meredithian sonnets stretches before us for another two or three decades; and he has attempted with success the middle-length poem, especially in 'A Kumquat for John Keats' included here. The same can be said of others. Peter Scupham has never been entirely happy with the limitations of the lyric; he has gone for loose sequences, tighter sequences of a baroque complexity, until his latest book can be read almost as one long poem. Andrew Waterman's huge *Out for the Elements*, in exacting stanzas borrowed from Pushkin, is part of a quite remarkably copious *oeuvre*. And while Harrison,

Scupham and Waterman are not exactly typical in the scope and range of their work, several of those included here have written an extensive body of poetry and prose. With Frank Kuppner, who makes his debut in this anthology, and Alison Brackenbury, we have seen only the very tip of the iceberg.

A widespread dissatisfaction with the short lyric mode is part of a wider dissatisfaction with the unqualified first person 'I', and only a few of these poets use the 'I' in any but a tentative and defensive spirit. The *persona* does overtime, or the poet arranges voices rather than speaking himself. Shades of Clough, perhaps, quite as much as Browning. The arrangement of voices is more than a game for an innovative writer like John Ash (the one poet here who has a claim to the title 'post-modern'). The play of registers and tones might at first seem to aspire to the dramatic, but in fact it is more a musical model that lies behind Ash's procedures: modulations and recurrences rather than punch-lines, a strategy which avoids statement and locates the poem's meaning inextricably in the very languages of the poem. Dramatic models do, however, seem to lie behind the work of Harrison, who has written for the stage and whose classical training makes him our most effective traditional rhetorician; and also behind the work of James Fenton. Contemporary European fiction has left a mark on the truncated stories and vignettes of the youngest poet here, Michael Hofmann.

The poets who look most eccentric in this anthology are probably those—Dick Davis, Robert Wells and Clive Wilmer in particular—who are resolutely traditional in their approach to the craft of poetry, and yet whose precisions make them in some respects most radical. They deploy abstractions in contexts which give them back proper specific gravity; they experiment with metre in ways which bring their language closer to the experiences that compel them. In Davis's poems we find notes of civility that have not been struck for a long time in English poetry; in Robert Wells's poems there is a physicality and immediacy which are made possible because the language does not surrender to its occasion but sets out to master it. At a time when there is a premium on 'effect' in poetry, their work is a salutary tonic, reminding us that there are vital areas of our tradition still accessible to the tactful writer who is willing to efface himself with *pietas* in the service of his subjects.

Recently, much has been made of the revival of 'narrative'. The term should be regarded with suspicion. There *are* narrative poems such as Andrew Motion's *Independence* and Alison Brackenbury's *Dreams of Power*. But some of what is presented as narrative is merely anecdote.

The poet tells a story borrowed from the experience of someone else —a relation, a friend, an outcast—for which he is not finally responsible. Why have poets had recourse to anecdote to such an extent? The anecdote-poem is another means of avoiding first-person statement. For the writer reticent about the authority of his own experience or distrustful of the 'subjective', it is a mode of extension, a way of exploiting 'important' themes, bringing in dungeons, censors, oppression, political and historical turbulences (Enclosure, Empire, etc.). The resonances are there for the borrowing. Anecdote also entertains. But when a plot structure does service for poetic form, and the term 'narrative' is used to dignify a story told in short lines, one senses a minor crisis in critical terminology. It is part of a wider crisis: other words (new and old) do rather heavy unskilled labour in contemporary criticism. They hinder rather than ease the way for the general reader. Towards the end of last century, critical discourse was sometimes limply impressionistic; nowadays it can be stiff with one of several ideologies. Both extremes are unhappy for poetry, which can profit only from the companionship of lucid criticism.

Towards the end of our century, we too have our characteristic dying falls in verse; our political helplessnesses after 1968 and the years of war in Northern Ireland; the difficulty of God (how secular my generation is, compared with the one that stretches from R. S. Thomas to Geoffrey Hill, a generation for which 'the matter of the spirit' is still of real, if often vexed, concern); and decadence in some poets' attitudes towards subject-matter and the metaphorical liberties they can take with a given world.

Of course, we have not been *exactly* here before. But those readers who are dazzled by the novelty and coherence of the poetry of this generation take a very short or a partial view, it seems to me. What is novel is the degree of positive incoherence, the absence of general poetic trends. For the poet, many roads are open. Some are fashionable roads, and on them there are the traffic jams and tail-backs which get into the news. But on the quieter and more difficult roads—those travelled by Tony Harrison, Derek Mahon, Dick Davis, James Fenton— I detect no followers. Their best work arranges, deepens, enchants; it is the fruit of specific skills, specific experiences, specified occasions.

To appreciate the range of recent work here, no doubt new readers will have to reform their taste a little: to listen to the ordered sounds the poets make, as well as do those things the classroom teaches: to watch images and to paraphrase. The skills most wanting among younger readers are aural skills; and the deficiency of such skills severely hampers an aptitude for discriminating and pleasurable reading. The reader whose ears have not been attuned by a reading of the poetry of the past will find the best poetry of the present perplexing, and may be taken in by vendors of novelties. What is new in poetry is always the way the elements are combined. There are seldom new elements. Poets and critics who insist on the novel primacy of one element—'narrative' or 'metaphor', for instance—over the others as marking a timely enrichment of poetry, as defining a 'decisive shift of sensibility', exclude a great deal, and constrain that catholic critical discourse which is part of the context in which good writing occurs.

# PETER SCUPHAM

## THE NONDESCRIPT

I am plural. My intents are manifold:
I see through many eyes. I am fabulous.

I assimilate the suffering of monkeys:
Tiger and musk-ox are at my disposal.

My ritual is to swallow a pale meat
Prepared by my ignorant left hand.

It is my child's play to untie a frog,
Humble further the worm and dogfish.

When I comb the slow pond,
I shake out a scurf of tarnished silver;

When I steer the long ship to the stones,
A brown sickness laps at the cliff's foot.

Shreds of fur cling to my metalled roads,
Old plasters seeping a little blood.

I dress and powder the wide fields:
They undergo my purgatorial fires.

Come with me. I will shake the sky
And watch the ripe birds tumble.

It requires many deaths to ease
The deep cancer in my marrowbones.

I have prepared a stone inheritance.
It flourishes beneath my fertile tears.

# PREHISTORIES

## 1

Adrowse, my pen trailed on, and a voice spoke:
'Now, you must read us "Belknap".' My book was open.

I saw their faces; there were three of them,
Each with a certain brightness in her eyes.

I would read 'Belknap'. Then a gardener's shears
Snipped fatefully my running thread of discourse.

And in my indices, no poem upon which
I could confer this honorary title.

Foundering in dictionaries and gazetteers,
I came there: Belas Knap, a chambered tomb.

The lips are closed upon the withered barrow:
A dummy portal, a slant lintel hung

Beneath a scalp of ruinous grass, her walls
A packed mosaic of blurred syllables.

## 2

Entering is a deployment of small silences,
Frail collusions and participations.

A scrape of some sad traffic on the ear,
Bird song at her old insouciance,

I pull these down into an underworld
Of images alive in their dark shelter.

Such corridors are tacitly inscribed:
Do not abandon hope here, but desire.

When old men's voices stumble down the lane,
They too must be my dry accompaniment.

There is a shrinking in each new encounter,
A heaviness attendant on the work.

The vanished bone sings in her shallow alcove,
Making a sacred and astounding music.

Ghosts are a poet's working capital.
They hold their hands out from the further shore.


3

The spirit leans her bleak peninsulas:
Our granite words loosen towards the sea,

Or hold, by some wild artifice, at Land's End.
The Merry Maidens dance their come ye all,

Keeping time to the piper's cold slow-motion,
Their arms linked against the lichenous Sabbath.

And a menhir, sharp-set, walled about
By a dirt-farm, a shuffle of lean cows,

Accepts, as of right, our casual veneration,
All fertile ceremonies of birth and death.

I see you standing, the new life quick in you,
Poised on Chun Quoit into the flying sky.

There, in that grave the wind has harrowed clean,
Our children crouch, clenched in a fist of stone.


# WIND AND ABSENCE

Down wind, down wind, a soft sweep of hours
Trawling in time. My pulse races into darkness.

Adrift, I draw your absence close about me;
Take the small ghosts of your hands to mine.

Your voice, your smile: such *son et lumière*.
My nerves conduct you round my floodlit bones.

Certain salt-water fools pester my eyes:
I stub them out with rough, dumb fingers.

The wind rehearses idle punishments,
Shaking a crush of unrecorded leaves.

A long–dead singer clears his ashen throat:
You creep his old cold music into life.

Poems bite on their pains. Dismayed, I know
The lines are scored in poker-work: black fire.

The haunted room trembles at your insistency.
Small, ghostly hands, allay the air's distress

As wind gathers, menacing our naked spaces
In dead languages of distance and rejection.


# EFFACEMENTS

The steady cedars levelling the shade
Bend in the waters of each diamond pane.
Furred cusp and sill: other effacements made
Where the armorial glass in bronze and grain
    Stiffens a lily on the clouded sun.
    The lozenge hatchments of the porch floor run

Far out to grass. The grave Palladians
Have gone to seed, long genealogies
Dissolve beneath their wet and gentry stones;
The leaves lie shaken from the family trees.
    As kneeling putti, children from the Hall
    Are playing marbles on the mildewed wall.

The letters and the memoirs knew His will;
All Spring contracted to the one hushed room.
White swelling grew, he passed the cup, lay still;
To the bed's foot she saw the dark spades come.
    They made such vanishings their deodands;
    The earth records what the earth understands.

Queen's May beneath his firstborn coffin lid:
A lock of hair reserved, a brief pray said.
'Each lifeless hand extended by his side
Clasped thy fresh blossoms when his bloom was fled.'
    Pain wrote in copperplate one epigraph,
    Then sealed the album's crimson cenotaph.

Behind locked doors, an audience of hymnals.
Tablet and effigy rehearse their lines
To cold light falling in a cold chancel.
Grammarians at their Roman slates decline
    Each proper noun. Bells close on a plain song.
    All speak here with an adult, eheu tongue.

But those frail mounds, brushed low by ancient rain,
Their markers undiscerned in the half-light . . . ?
The last of day ghosts out a window; stains
The scarred porch wall, whose rough and honeyed weight
    Glows from the shade: stones so intangible
    A child might slip between them, bones and all.

# MARGINALIA

1

*Leaf from a French Bible* Circa *1270*
*Villeneuve-les-Avignons*

A single leaf. Deuteronomy.
The untrimmed vellum keeps its pinholes;
Guide-lines rest uncancelled.

Under the Uncials' lantern capitals,
Whose gentler reds and blues are hung
On vines of gossamer,

The blocked ink scorches on the page.
Textus quadratus: bent feet hook
The linked chains of the Word.

A slant-cut nib works on; the skin
Takes texture. God is woven close —
The figure in the carpet.

And at the margin, crabbed, contracted,
Lies evidence the page was read. No more.
A commentary on silence.

Wind in the cloister's lost mandala;
Cold hands re-cut the blunted quill.
Somehwere, the child Dante

Sees Folco Portinari's quiet daughter,
And all the formal rose of heaven opens
On the one slender stem.


2

*Jeremy Taylor:*
*The Rule and Exercise of Holy Dying, 1663*

Grey flowers in their pleated urns,
The frozen spray, the flying skull,
And the dark words' processional.

Thomas Langley Purcell. His book.
About the Doctor's text extends
A glossolalia of hands.

Where the Baroque moves into night
These light and active fingers thrive,
Cuffs frilled, the mood indicative.

And one small coffin, monogrammed,
Nibbed out with nail-heads. Nota Bene.
The period of human glory.

The sepia glitters and grows pale,
Memorial of a heart at school;
Praeceptor, student, work there still.

'You can go no whither but
You tread upon a dead man's bones.'
I read you still between the lines.

A shut book — as a church door closed
On congregations known, unknown,
On tireless monitors of stone.

3

*Rider's British Merlin, 1778*

The almanac's green vellum skin is rubbed
To duckpond water. There, stub fingers felt
For the cold patina of a broken clasp.

Under the stitching and the rough-cut ties
The 'Useful Verities fitting all Capacities
In the Islands of Great Britain's Monarchy'

Hold their rusticities of red and black,
Pragmatic as all northern frost and mud.
Look to your Sheep. Eat no gross Meats. Sow Pease.

The rightful owner still some revenant
From foundered England, scrawling his Receits,
Juggling his Honny, Daffy Elixir, Terpedine,

For the Rumatis, the Coff, For Nervious Complaints.
'Jesus Jesus Jesus My teeth doth ake
And Jesus said Take Up thy Cross and Follow me.'

No name. And yet by sleight of charm and simple,
In language stripped by dumb hedge-carpentry,
Some churchyard clay turned Goodfellow survives

The Bale-fires leaping out at Coalbrookdale,
The long-defeated children, all the sparrows
God seemed to have no eyes for when they fell.


# THE DOVES

'Eheu, eheu,' doves follow to the close of March:
The white one blossoms, as on a Tree of Jesse,
Where the scaled mullions part the black-silk lights
On the tower lancet. Sun eases the winter skin,
Firing her reds and yellows under membranes
Traced out by birdsong passing sweet and high
Through all the churchyard trees. Boughs come adrift
Over the splayed sword-work of spring flowers,
The superscriptions — Ballance, Mynott, Mellodey.

Rough marble lets fly her cold scintillae.
What were you for, who lie here in accord
With the erosions of this further season?
Light shivers from drubbed grass; then the stillness,
And the doves, as doves do, mourn, mourn.


# TRENCROM

The salt brushed pelt of trees could hide them:
Ogres and witches who play pitch and toss
Or loose an apronful of clumsy pebbles
To stun the landscape into graves and kitchens.
Their lives are long and legendary as bones,
Their sleep deeper and harder than our sleep.

Quieter the gods of estuary and sand,
Holding their smoky fingers to our lips
And easing middle distance into distance;
Bruising the grass to a slow stain of brown,
Shimmering our goose-skin with mist fingers.

The dead men leave their sunken gates unposted.
An age of iron rusts into a silence
Made luminous, as evening light discloses
A cold intimacy we had not looked for.

As if even the stones could drop their veils,
Discovering some life under their scarred rind,
Or words form from a circumference of wind.

Rocks breeding chill in deep interstices.
The ferns darkening, and the lizards gone.

We are moving under, and beyond the hill.


# ATLANTIC

There's loss in the Atlantic sky
Smoking her course from sea to sea,
Whitening an absence, till the eye

Aches dazed above the mainmast tree.
  The fuchsia shakes her lanterns out;
  The stiffening winds must go about.

Green breakers pile across the moor
Whose frayed horizons ebb and flow;
Grass hisses where the garden floor
Pulls to a wicked undertow.
  A ragged Admiral of the Red
  Beats up and down the flowerbed.

Granite, unmoving and unmoved,
Rides rough-shod our peninsula
Where curlews wait to be reproved
And petals of a hedge-rose star
  The beaten path. Uncoloured rain
  Rattles her shrouds upon the pane.

Beyond the ledges of the foam
A dog seal sways an oilskin head;
The Carracks worked old luggers home,
Black rock commemorates the dead.
  The sea shouts nothing, and the shores
  Break to a tumult of applause.

But mildewed on the parlour wall,
The Thomas Coutts, East Indiaman,
Enters Bombay. Her mainsail haul
Swells to the light. A rajah sun
  Accepts her flying ribbon still,
  Though bracken darkens on the hill.

A peg-leg cricket limps the floor.
See, China Poll and Jack link hands.
Blown long ago on a lee-shore,
His hour-glass run on to the sands,
  He bids her wipe her eye, for soft,
  A cherub watches from aloft

Who knows our hulk is anchored fast,
Though timbers fret in their decline.
The cattle heads are overcast;
The gutter shakes her glittering line.
  Rage at the door. Winds twist and drown.
  We founder as the glass goes down.

# THE CHAIN

Above us, numbing all our dreams with tales
Of bad islands, infestations of gulls,
The metal broadsides of our great ark tower.
There hangs the chain: sealed rounds of iron
Whose chafe and rust, they say, ensure our freedom.
Paid out with its reel of swollen fathoms
Something of us gropes there, where deeper, deeper,
The hook works pain into a muddy craw.

Allow us good days, when, in certain lights,
Waves ease links to invisibility,
Gleam slips from gleam, all the lithe flexure
Polishes to a haze of blue and pearl.
So the stump dwarves, gold-beating out Sif's hair,
Worked that obdurate element to a nature
Divine and animal: this was craft-work,
A clasp tendered by their slavish hands.

Our Pilot, arms akimbo, saturnine,
Rigged out in steeple hat and greasy frock-coat,
Stares back at us from his ancestral eyes.

# THE BEACH

And Langland told how heaven could not keep love;
It overflowed that room, took flesh, became
Light as a linden-leaf, sharp as a needle.

Today, the stone pavilion throws a window
Into the morning, that great strength of silver
Shawled from the climbing sun, and on four children
Alive to rippled beach and rippled water
Swaying their metalled lights in amity.

Hands build an airy house of meetings, partings,
Over a confluence of the elements
Here, where there is neither sex nor name,
Only the skirmishes of dark and bright,
Clear surfaces replenished and exchanged.

Black dancing in a hall of spacious mirrors,
Far voices, and the hush of sea on sand
Light as a linden-leaf, sharp as a needle.


# THE ORNAMENTAL HERMITS

Veiled melancholy, mid-lay accidie,
   Improvings of the landskip sheathed in rain:
We dwell, not live, shifting from knee to knee
   In robes as uncanonical as plain,
Nodding, like Homer, over knucklebones,
   (Cold vertebrae a starwork on the floor)
Serviced by birdsong: vespers, compline, nones —
   The cycles of unalterable law.
Our eremitic dirt, our nails prepare
   A mortification close to Godliness;
Under the tangled prayer-mats of our hair
   Each sours into his mimic wilderness.

The Desert Fathers, locked into each cell,
   Knew all the pleasures that retirements bring:
The succubus, the tumbling insect-hell,
   Assault of breast and thorax, thigh and wing.
Our bark-house windows, open to the sky,
   Show vellum faces, blind-stamped and antique:
A glaze of rigor-mortis at the eye,
   A tear-drop crocodiled upon the cheek.
The unread Testament aslant each knee
   Will not dispel the simple moth and rust
Corrupting us, degree by slow degree,
   Into the scattered frictions of the dust.

We beck, we hoist our creaking arms, we nod,
   Blessing processionals of cane and fan,
Attuned to Paley and his tick-tock God
   Or swung in gimbals pre-Copernican.
And who dare call our observation vain?
   The celebration, not the celebrant,
Will keep the ancient order clear and plain;
   We too are arks of His great covenant:
God's weathercocks, upon his axle pinned,
   The beads of an industrious rosary,
Tibetan prayer-wheels turning on the wind,
   Imprisoned things which float the bright dove free.

# MADELON
*Part One of 'Notes from a War Diary, H. J. B. 1914–19'*

This is the song the poilus sing,
  Madelon! Madelon! Madelon!
'Et chacun lui raconte une histoire,
  Une histoire à sa façon.'

A captured goat in the Canteen Car,
  Driven by 'Darky' Robinson,
Magpies, poppies and marguerites,
  Crosses are wreathed among the corn.

'Glorious weather all the time',
  (Shelling of Ablois St Martin,)
To a walnut tree, by the Villa des Fleurs,
  Faux–Fresnay, Vaux, Courcemain.

He's never seen two prettier girls,
  With manners to match, pink dresses on,
Little Monique, Jacqueline,
  Mme Pinard — or is it Pinant?

And a stolen flight with Paul Scordel,
  (Back in time for parade at 9,)
'Regardez à gauche pendant la spirale',
  (A mustard-yellow A.R. Type 1.)

'La servante est jeune et gentille,
  Légère comme un papillon,
Comme son vin so oeuil pétille,
  Nous l'appelons La Madelon.'

But seven die at the Aerodrome,
  (Spads, appareil de chasse, monoplane,)
'Forget your sweethearts, forget your wives',
  A Bréguet dives on a Voisin.

'Adieu Champagne, Villa des Fleurs',
  To the Airmen and the waving corn,
The convoy leaves the little Square,
  Beaumont, St Omer and Hesdin.

'Hope for a revoir bientôt',
   Thirty-eight years, to the day, in June,
Back 'en passant' to the Villa des Fleurs,
   To Faux-Fresnay and Courcemain.

Canterbury bells in the garden still,
   The house closed up, the shutters on,
And Monique dead at twelve years old,
   And the walnut tree cut down and gone.

What was the song the poilus sang?
   Madelon! Madelon! Madelon!
'Et chacun lui raconte une histoire,
   Une histoire à sa façon.'

# TONY HARRISON

## THOMAS CAMPEY AND THE COPERNICAN SYSTEM

The other day all thirty shillings' worth
Of painfully collected waste was blown
Off the heavy handcart high above the earth,
And scattered paper whirled around the town.

*The earth turns round to face the sun in March*
He said, resigned, *it's bound to cause a breeze*.
Familiar last straws. His back's strained arch
Questioned the stiff balance of his knees.

Thomas Campey, who, in each demolished home,
Cherished a Gibbon with a gilt-worked spine,
Spengler and Mommsen, and a huge, black tome
With Latin titles for his own decline:

*Tabes dorsalis*; veins like flex, like fused
And knotted flex, with a cart on the cobbled road,
He drags for life old clothing, used
Lectern bibles and cracked Copeland Spode,

Marie Corelli, Ouida and Hall Caine
And texts from Patience Strong in tortoise frames.
And every pound of this dead weight is pain
To Thomas Campey (Books) who often dreams

Of angels in white crinolines all dressed
To kill, of God as Queen Victoria who grabs
Him by the scruff and shoves his body pressed
Quite straight again under St Anne's slabs.

And around Victoria Regina the Most High
Swathed in luminous smokes like factories,
These angels serried in a dark, Leeds sky
Chanting *Angina — a, Angina Pectoris*.

Keen winter is the worst time for his back,
Squeezed lungs and damaged heart; just one
More sharp turn of the earth, those knees will crack
And he will turn his warped spine on the sun.

Leeds! Offer thanks to that Imperial Host,
Squat on its thrones of Ormus and of Ind,
For bringing Thomas from his world of dust
To dust, and leisure of the simplest kind.

## THE NUPTIAL TORCHES

*These human victims, chained and burning at the stake, were the blazing
torches which lighted the monarch to his nuptial couch.*
—J. L. Motley, *The Rise of the Dutch Republic*

Fish gnaw the Flushing capons, hauled from fleeced
Lutheran Holland, for tomorrow's feast.
The Netherlandish lengths, the Dutch heirlooms,
That might have graced my movements and my groom's
Fade on the fat sea's bellies where they hung
Like cover-sluts. Flesh, wet linen wrung
Bone dry in a washerwoman's raw, red,
Twisting hands, bed-clothes off a lovers'.bed,
Falls off the chains. At Valladolid
It fell, flesh crumpled like a coverlid.

Young Carlos de Sessa stripped was good
For a girl to look at and he spat like wood
Green from the orchards for the cooking pots.
Flames ravelled up his flesh into dry knots
And he cried at the King: *How can you stare
On such agonies and not turn a hair?*
The King was cool: My friend, *I'd drag the logs
Out to the stake for my own son, let dogs
Get at his testes for his sins; auto-da-fés
Owe no paternity to evil ways.*
Cabrera leans against the throne, guffaws
And jots down to the Court's applause
Yet another of the King's *bon mots.*

O yellow piddle in fresh fallen snow —
Dogs on the Guadarramas . . . dogs. Their souls
Splut through their pores like porridge holes.
They wear their skins like cast-offs. Their skin grows
Puckered round the knees like rumpled hose.

Doctor Ponce de la Fuente, you,
Whose gaudy, straw-stuffed effigy in lieu

Of members hacked up in the prison, burns
Here now, one sacking arm drops off, one turns
A stubble finger and your skull still croons
Lascivious catches and indecent tunes;
And croaks: *Ashes to ashes, dust to dust.*
*Pray God be with you in your lust.*
And God immediately is, but such a one
Whose skin stinks like a herring in the sun,
Huge from confinement in a filthy gaol,
Crushing the hooping on my farthingale.

O Holy Mother, Holy Mother, Ho–
ly Mother Church, whose melodious, low
Labour-moans go through me as you bear
These pitch-stained children to the upper air,
Let them lie still tonight, no crowding smoke
Condensing back to men float in and poke
Their charcoaled fingers at our bed, and let
Me be his pleasure, though Philip sweat
At his rhythms and use those hateful tricks
They say he feels like after heretics.

O let the King be gentle and not loom
Like Torquemada in the torture room,
Those wiry Spanish hairs, these nuptial nights,
Crackling like lit tapers in his tights,
His seed like water spluttered off hot stone.
Maria, whose dark eyes very like my own
Shine on such consummations, Maria bless
My Philip just this once with gentleness.

The King's cool knuckles on my smoky hair!

*Mare Mediterraneum, la mer, la mer*
That almost got him in your gorge with sides
Of feastmeats, you must flush this scared bride's
Uterus with scouring salt. O cure and cool
The scorching birthmarks of his branding–tool.

Sweat chills my small breasts and limp hands.

They curled like foetuses, *maman*, and cried.

His crusted tunics crumple as he stands:

*Come, Isabella.* God *is satisfied.*

# ON NOT BEING MILTON
*for Sergio Vieira & Armando Guebuza* (Frelimo)

Read and committed to the flames, I call
these sixteen lines that go back to my roots
my *Cahier d'un retour au pays natal*
my growing black enough to fit my boots.

The stutter of the scold out of the branks
of condescension, class and counter-class
thickens with glottals to a lumpen mass
of Ludding morphemes closing up their ranks.
Each swung cast-iron Enoch★ of Leeds stress
clangs a forged music on the frames of Art,
the looms of owned language smashed apart!

Three cheers for mute ingloriousness!

Articulation is the tongue-tied's fighting.
In the silence round all poetry we quote
Tidd the Cato Street conspirator who wrote:

*Sir, I Ham a very Bad Hand at Righting.*


# CLASSICS SOCIETY
(*Leeds Grammar School 1552–1952*)

*the grace of Tullies eloquence doth excell
any Englishmans tongue . . . my barbarous stile.*

The tongue our leaders use to cast their spell
was once denounced as 'rude', 'gross', 'base' and 'vile'.

How fortunate we are who've come so far!

We boys can take old Hansards and translate
the British Empire as S.P.Q.R.
but nothing demotic or too up-too-date,

---

★ An 'Enoch' is an iron sledge-hammer used by the Luddites to smash the frames which were also made by the same Enoch Taylor of Marsden. The cry was: Enoch made them, Enoch shall break them!

and certainly not how I speak at home.
Not Hansard standards, and if Antoninus
spoke like delinquent Latin back in Rome
he'd probably get gamma double minus.

And so the lad who gets the alphas works
the hardest in his class at his translation
and finds good Ciceronian for Burke's:

*a dreadful schism in the British nation.*

# NATIONAL TRUST

Bottomless pits. There's one in Castleton,
and stout upholders of our law and order
one day thought its depth worth wagering on
and borrowed a convict hush-hush from his warder
and winched him down; and back, flayed, grey, mad, dumb.

Not even a good flogging made him holler.

O gentlemen, a better way to plumb
the depths of Britain's dangling a scholar,
say, here at the booming shaft at Towanroath,
now National Trust, a place where they got tin,
those gentlemen who silenced the men's oath
and killed the language that they swore it in.

The dumb go down in history and disappear
and not one gentleman's been brought to book:

*Mes den hep tavas a-gollas y dyr*

(Cornish) — 'the tongueless man gets his land took.'

# BOOK ENDS

Baked the day she suddenly dropped dead
we chew it slowly that last apple pie.

Shocked into sleeplessness you're scared of bed.
We never could talk much, and now don't try.

*You're like book ends, the pair of you,* she'd say,
*Hog that grate, say nothing, sit, sleep, stare . . .*

The 'scholar' me, you, worn out on poor pay,
only our silence made us seem a pair.

Not as good for staring in, blue gas,
too regular each bud, each yellow spike.

A night you need my company to pass
and she not here to tell us we're alike!

Your life's all shattered into smithereens.

Back in our silences and sullen looks,
for all the Scotch we drink, what 's still between 's
not the thirty or so years, but books, books, books.


# CONTINUOUS

James Cagney was the one up both our streets.
His was the only art we ever shared.
A gangster film and choc ice were the treats
that showed about as much love as he dared.

He'd be my own age now in '49!
The hand that glinted with the ring he wore,
*his* father's, tipped the cold bar into mine
just as the organist dropped through the floor.

He's on the platform lowered out of sight
to organ music, this time on looped tape,
into a furnace with a blinding light
where only his father's ring will keep its shape.

I wear it now to Cagneys on my own
and sense my father's hands cupped round my treat —

they feel as though they've been chilled to the bone
from holding my ice cream all through *White Heat*.

# TIMER

Gold survives the fire that's hot enough
to make you ashes in a standard urn.
An envelope of coarse official buff
contains your wedding ring which wouldn't burn.

Dad told me I'd to tell them at St. James's
that the ring should go in the incinerator.
That 'eternity' inscribed with both their names is
his surety that they'd be together, 'later'.

I signed for the parcelled clothing as the son,
this cardy, apron, pants, bra, dress —

the clerk phoned down: *6–8–8–3–1?*
*Has she still her ring on?* (Slight pause) *Yes!*

It's on my warm palm now, your burnished ring!

I feel your ashes, head, arms, breasts, womb, legs,
sift through its circle slowly, like that thing
you used to let me watch to time the eggs.

# ART & EXTINCTION

*'When I hear of the destruction of a species I feel as if all the works of some
great writer had perished.'*
Theodore Roosevelt 1899

I

*The Birds of America: John James Audubon (1785–1851)*

The struggle to preserve once spoken words
from already too well-stuffed taxonomies
is a bit like Audubon's when painting birds,
whose method an admirer said was this:
*Kill 'em, wire 'em, paint 'em, kill a fresh 'un!*

The plumage even of the brightest faded.
The artist had to shoot in quick succession
till all the feathers were correctly shaded.

Birds don't pose for picures when alive!
Audubon's idea of restraint,
doing the Pelican, was 25
dead specimens a day for *one* in paint.

By using them do we save words or not?

As much as Audubon's art could save a,
say, godwit, or a grackle, which he shot
and then saw 'multiplied by Havell's graver'.


II

*Standards*
*in hopeful anticipation of the bicentenary of the national emblem of the*
*United States of America*
Haliaaetus Falco Leucocephalus, 1782–1982

'Our standard with the eagle stands for us.
It waves in the breeze in almost every clime.'

(The flag, not *Falco Leucocephalus*
poised in its dying on the brink of time!)

Rejecting Franklin's turkey for a bird that *flies*
Congress chose the soaring eagle, called
for its conspicuous white head, 'the bald'.

Now the turkey's thriving and the eagle dies!

When the last stinks in its eyrie, or falls slow,
when the very last bald eagle goes the way
of all the unique fauna, it won't know
the Earth it plummets to 's the USA.

But will still wing over nations as the ghost
on money, and the mountainous US Post,

much as sunlight shining through the British pound
showed PEACE with her laurels, white on a green ground.

III

*Loving Memory*
for Teresa Stratas

The fosses where Caractacus fought Rome
blend with grey bracken and become a blur
above the Swedish Nightingale's last home.

Somehow my need for you makes me seek her.

The Malverns darken as the dusk soaks in.
The rowan berries' dark red glaze grows dull.
The harvest moon's scraped silver and bruised tin
is only one night off from being full.

Death keeps all hours, but graveyards close at nights.
I hurry past the Malvern Hospital
where a nurse goes round small wards and puts on lights
and someone there 's last night begins to fall.

'The oldest rocks this earth can boast', these hills,
packed with extinction, make me burn for you.

I ask two women leaving with dead daffodils:
*Where's Jenny Lind's grave, please?* They both say: *Who?*


IV

*Looking up*
for Philip, Terry, and Will Sharpe and the bicentenary of the birth of
Peter Mark Roget (1779–1869)

All day till it grows dark I sit and stare
over Herefordshire hills and into Wales.
Reflections of red coals thrown on the air
blossom to brightness as the daylight fails.

An uncharred cherry flaunts a May of flames.
Like chaffinches and robins tongues of fire
flit with the burden of Creation's names
but find no new apostles to inspire.

Bar a farmhouse TV aerial or two,
the odd red bus, the red Post Office van,
this must have been exactly Roget's view,
good Dr. Roget, the *Thesaurus* man.

Roget died here, but 90 when he died
of natural causes, twice as old as me.

Of his six synonyms for suicide
I set myself alight with safe suttee.


V

*Killing Time*

Among death-protected creatures in a case,
"The Earth's Endangered Species" on display
at a jam-packed terminal at JFK,
killing time again, I see my face
with Hawksbill Turtle, scrimshawed spermwhale bone,
the Margay of the family *Felidae,*
that, being threatened, cost the earth to buy.

And now with scientists about to clone
the long-haired mammoth back from Soviet frost,
my reflection's on the species the World's lost,
or will be losing in a little while,
which, as they near extinction, grow in worth,
the leopard, here a bag and matching purse,
the dancing shoes that were Nile crocodile,

the last *Felis Pardalis* left on Earth,

the poet preserved beneath deep permaverse.


VI

*t'ark*

Silence and poetry have their own reserves.
The numbered creatures flourish less and less.
A language near extinction best preserves
the deepest grammar of our nothingness

Not only dodo, oryx and great auk
waddled on their tod to t'monster ark,
but 'leg', 'night', 'origin' in crushed people's talk,
tongues of fire last witnessed mouthing: *dark*!

Now when the future couldn't be much darker,
there being fewer epithets for sun,
and Cornish and the Togoland *restsprache*
name both the animals and hunter's gun,
celebrate before things go too far
Papua's last reported manucode,
the pygmy hippo of the Cote d'Ivoire,
and Upper Guinea's oviparous toad —

(or mourn in Latin their imminent death,
then translate these poems into *cynghanedd*.)


VII

*Dark Times*

*That the Peppered Moth* was white and now is dark 's
a lesson in survival for Mankind.

Around the time Charles Darwin had declined
the dedication of *Das Kapital* by Marx
its predators could spot it on the soot,
but Industrial Revolution and Evolution taught
the moth to black its looks and not get caught
where all of Nature perished, or all but.

When lichens lighten some old smoke-grimed trees
and such as Yorkshire's millstacks now don't burn
and fish nose waters, stagnant centuries,
can *Biston Carbonaria* relearn,

if Man's awakened consciousness succeeds
in turning all these tides of blackness back
and diminishing the need for looking black,

to flutter white again above new Leeds?

VIII

*The Birds of America: Weeki Wachee*

Duds doomed to join the dodo: the dugong,
talonless eagles, croc, gimp manatee,
here courtesy Creation's generous strong
the losers of thinned jungle and slicked sea.

Many 's the proud chieftain used to strut
round shady clearings in dark festooned teak
with twenty cockatoo tails on his nut,
macaw plumes a la mode, rainforest chic.

Such gladrag gaudies safe in quarantine
and spared at least their former jungle fate
of being blowpiped for vain primitives to preen
now race a tightrope on one roller skate.

A tanned sophomore, these ghettoed birds' Svengali,
shows glad teeth, evolved for smiling, as macaws
perform their deft Darwinian finale
by hoisting the Stars and Stripes for our applause.

# A KUMQUAT FOR JOHN KEATS

Today I found the right fruit for my prime,
not orange, not tangelo, and not lime,
nor moon-like globes of grapefruit that now hang
outside our bedroom, nor tart lemon's tang
(though last year full of bile and self-defeat
I wanted to believe no life was sweet)
nor the tangible sunshine of the tangerine,
and no incongruous citrus ever seen
at greengrocers' in Newcastle or Leeds
mis-spelt by the spuds and mud-caked swedes,
a fruit an older poet might substitute
for the grape John Keats thought fit to be Joy's fruit,
when, two years before he died, he tried to write
how Melancholy dwelled inside Delight,
and if he'd known the citrus that I mean
that's not orange, lemon, lime or tangerine,
I'm pretty sure that Keats, though he had heard
'of candied apple, quince and plum and gourd'

instead of 'grape against the palate fine'
would have, if he'd known it, plumped for mine,
this Eastern citrus scarcely cherry size
he'd bite just once and then apostrophize
and pen one stanza how the fruit had all
the qualities of fruit before the Fall,
but in the next few lines be forced to write
how Eve's apple tasted at the second bite,
and if John Keats had only lived to be,
because of extra years, in need like me,
at 42 he'd help me celebrate
that Micanopy kumquat that I ate
whole, straight off the tree, sweet pulp and sour skin —
or was it sweet outside, and sour within?
For however many kumquats that I eat
I'm not sure if it's flesh or rind that's sweet,
and being a man of doubt at life's mid-way
I'd offer Keats some kumquats and I'd say:
*You'll find that one part's sweet and one part's tart:*
*say where the sweetness or the sourness start.*

I find I can't, as if one couldn't say
exactly where the night became the day,
which makes for me the kumquat taken whole
best fruit, and metaphor, to fit the soul
of one in Florida at 42 with Keats
crunching kumquats, thinking, as he eats
the flesh, the juice, the pith, the pips, the peel,
that this is how a full life ought to feel,
its perishable relish prick the tongue,
when the man who savours life's no longer young,
the fruits that were his futures far behind.
Then it's the kumquat fruit expresses best
how days have darkness round them like a rind,
life has a skin of death that keeps its zest.

History, a life, the heart, the brain
flow to the taste buds and flow back again.
That decade or more past Keats's span
makes me an older not a wiser man,
who knows that it's too late for dying young,
but since youth leaves some sweetnesses unsung,
he's granted days and kumquats to express
Man's Being ripened by his Nothingness.
And it isn't just the gap of sixteen years,

a bigger crop of terrors, hopes and fears,
but a century of history on this earth
between John Keats's death and my own birth —
years like an open crater, gory, grim,
with bloody bubbles leering at the rim;
a thing no bigger than an urn explodes
and ravishes all silence, and all odes,
Flora asphyxiated by foul air
unknown to either Keats or Lemprière,
dehydrated Naiads, Dryad amputees
dragging themselves through slagscapes with no trees,
a shirt of Nessus fire that gnaws and eats
children half the age of dying Keats . . .

Now were you twenty five or six years old
when that fevered brow at last grew cold?
I've got no books to hand to check the dates.
My grudging but glad spirit celebrates
that all I've got to hand 's the kumquats, John,
the fruit I'd love to have your verdict on,
but dead men don't eat kumquats, or drink wine,
they shiver in the arms of Proserpine,
not warm in bed beside their Fanny Brawne,
nor watch her pick ripe grapefruit in the dawn
as I did, waking, when I saw her twist,
with one deft movement of a sunburnt wrist,
the moon that feebly lit our last night's walk
past alligator swampland, off its stalk.
I thought of moon-juice juleps when I saw,
as if I'd never seen the moon before,
the planet glow among the fruit, and its pale light
make each citrus on the tree its satellite.

Each evening when I reach to draw the blind
stars seem the light zest squeezed through night's black rind;
the night's peeled fruit the sun, juiced of its rays,
first stains, then streaks, then floods the world with days,
days, when the very sunlight made me weep,
days, spent like the nights in deep, drugged sleep,
days in Newcastle by my daughter's bed,
wondering if she, or I, weren't better dead,
days in Leeds, grey days, my first dark suit,
my mother's wreaths stacked next to Christmas fruit,
and days, like this in Micanopy. Days!

As strong sun burns away the dawn's grey haze
I pick a kumquat and the branches spray
cold dew in my face to start the day.
The dawn's molasses make the citrus gleam
still in the orchards of the groves of dream.

The limes, like Galway after weeks of rain,
glow with a greenness that is close to pain,
the dew-cooled surfaces of fruit that spent
all last night flaming in the firmament.
The new day dawns. O days! My spirit greets
the kumquat with the spirit of John Keats.
O kumquat, comfort for not dying young,
both sweet and bitter, bless the poet's tongue!
I burst the whole fruit chilled by morning dew
against my palate. Fine, for 42!

I search for buzzards as the air grows clear
and see them ride fresh thermals overhead.
Their bleak cries were the first sound I could hear
when I stepped at the start of sunrise out of doors,
and a noise like last night's bedsprings on our bed
from Mr Fowler sharpening farmers' saws.

# GILLIAN CLARKE

## JOURNEY

As far as I am concerned
We are driving into oblivion.
On either side there is nothing,
And beyond your driving
Shaft of light it is black.
You are a miner digging
For a future, a mineral
Relationship in the dark.
I can hear the darkness drip
From the other world where people
Might be sleeping, might be alive.

Certainly there are white
Gates with churns waiting
For morning, their cream standing.
Once we saw an old table
Standing square on the grass verge.
Our lamps swept it clean, shook
The crumbs into the hedge and left it.
A tractor too, beside a load
Of logs, bringing from a deeper
Dark a damp whiff of the fungoid
Sterility of the conifers.

Complacently I sit, swathed
In sleepiness. A door shuts
At the end of a dark corridor.
Ahead not a cat's eye winks
To deceive us with its green
Invitation. As you hurl us
Into the black contracting
Chasm, I submit like a blind
And folded baby, being born.

# DYDDGU REPLIES TO DAFYDD

All year in open places, underneath
   the frescoed forest ceiling,
   we have made ceremony
   out of this seasonal love.

Dividing the leaf-shade as divers white
   in green pools we rose to dry
   islands of sudden sun. Then
   love seemed generosity.

Original sin I whitened from your
   mind, my colours influenced
   your flesh, as sun on the floor
   and warm furniture of a church.

So did our season bloom in mild weather,
   reflected gold like butter
   under chins, repeatedly
   unfolding to its clock of seed.

Autumn, our forest room is growing cold.
   I wait, shivering, feeling a
   dropping sun, a coming dark,
   your heart changing the subject.

The season coughs as it falls, like a coal;
   the trees ache. The forest falls
   to ruin, a roofless minster
   where only two still worship.

Love still, like sun, a vestment, celebrates,
   its warmth about our shoulders.
   I dread the day when Dyddgu's once
   loved name becomes a common cloak.

Your touch is not so light. I grow heavy.
   I wait too long, grow anxious,
   note your changing gestures, fear
   desire's alteration.

The winter stars are flying and the owls
  sing. You are packing your songs
  in a sack, narrowing your
  words, as you stare at the road.

The feet of young men beat somewhere far off
  on the mountain. I would women
  had roads to tread in winter
  and other lovers waiting.

A raging rose all summer falls to snow,
  keeps its continuance in
  frozen soil. I must be patient
  for the breaking of the crust.

I must be patient that you will return
  when the wind whitens the tender
  underbelly of the March grass
  thick as pillows under the oaks.


# WATERFALL

We parked the car in a dusty village
That sat sideways on a hill over the coal.
We heard a rag and bone man
And a curlew. The sun for the first time
Put a warm hand across our shoulders
And touched our winter faces.

We saw summer, one lapwing to go.
Her mate was in the sky already,
Turning over, black, white-bellied,
While she, looking browner near the ground,
Tidied the winter from her crisp field.

We climbed the mountain, crossed the round
Of it, following the marshland down the gorge.
The water was gathering minutely everywhere
Knowing its place and its time were coming.

Down over the boulders in the death bed
Of an old river, through thin birches and oaks,

Going where the water went, into the multitude
Of the shouting streams, no longer speaking
To each other, silenced by what the water said.

Closer to crisis the air put cold silk
Against our faces and the cliffs streamed
With sun water, caging on every gilded
Ledge small things that flew by mistake
Into the dark spaces behind the rainbows.

The path led me under the fall to feel
The arc of the river and the mountain's exact
Weight; the roar of rain and lapwings
Leaving; water-beat, heart-fall in accord,
Curlew-call, child-cry on the drum's skin
Distinguished from the inmost thoughts of rivers.

We cage our response in the roar, defer
Decision while water falls. It gathers its life
On our behalf, leaps for us, its chords
Of change that curve across the cliffs
Are only, after all, an altering of level
To where it belongs, though the falling appals.

## EAST MOORS

At the end of a bitter April
the cherries flower at last in Penylan.
We notice the white trees and the flash
of sea with two blue islands beyond
the city, where the steelworks used to smoke.

I live in the house I was born in,
am accustomed to the sudden glow
of flame in the night sky, the dark sound
of something heavy dropped, miles off,
the smell of sulphur almost natural.

In Roath and Rumney now, washing strung
down the narrow gardens will stay clean.
Lethargy settles in front rooms and wives
have lined up little jobs for men to do.

A few men stay to see it through. Theirs
the bitterest time as rolling mills
make rubble. Demolition gangs
erase skylines whose hieroglyphs
recorded all our stories.

I am reminded of that Sunday
years ago when we brought the children
to watch two water cooling towers
blown up, recall the appalling void
in the sunlight, like a death.

On this first day of May an icy
rain is blowing through this town,
quieter, cleaner, poorer from today.
The cherries are in flower in Penylan.
Already over East Moors the sky whitens, blind.

# SIEGE

I waste the sun's last hour sitting here
at the kitchen window. Tea and a pile
of photographs to sort. Radio news
like smoke of conflagrations far away.
There isn't room for another petal
or leaf out there, this year of blossom.
Light dazzles the hedge roots underneath
the heavy shadows, burns the long grass.

> *I, in my father's arms in this garden,*
> *with dandelion hair. He, near forty,*
> *unaccustomed to the restlessness*
> *of a baby's energy. Small hands*
> *tear apart the photograph's composure.*
> *She pushes his chest to be let down*
> *where daisies embroider his new shoes.*

Perfumes and thorns are tearing
from the red may tree. Wild white morello
and a weeping cherry heavy in flower.
The lilac slowly shows. Small oaks spread
their gestures. Poplars glisten. Pleated green
splits black husks of ash. Magnolia

drops its wax. Forsythia
fallen like a yellow dress.
Underfoot daisies from a deep
original root burst the darkness.

> My mother, posing in a summer dress
> in the corn at harvest time. Her brothers
> shadowy middle distance figures
> stoop with pitchforks to lift the sheaves.
> Out of sight Captain, or Belle, head fallen
> to rest in the lee of the load, patient
> for the signal. Out of heart too the scare
> of the field far down from the sunstruck top
> of the load, and the lurch at the gate
> as we ditch and sway left down the lane.

The fallen sun lies low in the bluebells.
It is nearly summer. Midges hang
in the air. A wren is singing, sweet
in a lilac tree. Thrushes hunt the lawn,
eavesdrop for stirrings in the daisy roots.
The wren repeats his message distantly.
In a race of speedwell over grass
the thrushes are silently listening.
A yellow butterfly begins
its unsteady journey over the lawn.

The radio voices break and suddenly
the garden burns, is full of barking dogs.
A woman screams and gunsmoke blossoms
in the apple trees. Sheaves of fire
are scorching the grass and in my kitchen
is a roar of floors falling, machine guns.
The wren moves closer and repeats that song
of lust and burgeoning. Never clearer
the figures standing on the lawn, sharpnesses
of a yellow butterfly, almost there.

# THE WATER-DIVINER

His fingers tell water like prayer.
He hears its voice in the silence
through fifty feet of rock
on an afternoon still with drought.

Under an old tin bath, a stone,
an upturned can, his copper pipe
glints with discovery. We dip our hose
deep into the dark, sucking its dryness,

till suddenly the water answers,
not the little sound we know,
but a thorough bass too deep
for the naked ear, shouts through the hose

a word we could not say, or spell, or remember,
something like 'Dŵr . . . dŵr'.

# TAID'S FUNERAL

From a drawer, a scrap of creased cloth,
an infant's dress of yellowed Viyella
printed with daisies. And a day opens
suddenly as light. The sun is hot.
Grass grows cleanly to a chapel wall.
The stones are rough as a sheepdog's tongue
on the skin of two-year child.
They allow a fistful of white
gravel, chain her wrists with daisies.

Under the yew tree they lay Taid
in his box like a corm in the ground.

The lawn-mowers are out. Fears repeat
in a conversation of mirrors,
doll within doll; and that old man too small
at last to see, perfect, distinct as a seed.
My hands are cut by silver gravel.
There are dark incisions in the stalks
of the daisies made by a woman's nail.
A new dress stains green with their sap.

# SHEILA NA GIG AT KILPECK

Pain's a cup of honey in the pelvis.
She burns in the long, hot afternoon, stone
among the monstrous nursery faces
circling Kilpeck church. Those things we notice
as we labour distantly revolve
outside her perpetual calendar.
Men in the fields. Loads following the lanes,
strands of yellow hair caught in the hedges.

The afternoon turns round us.
The beat of the heart a great tongue in its bell,
a swell between bone cliffs; restlessness
that sets me walking; that second sight
of shadows crossing cornfields. We share
premonitions, are governed by moons
and novenas, sisters cooling our wrists
in the stump of a Celtic water stoup.

Not lust but long labouring
absorbs her, mother of the ripening
barley that swells and frets at its walls.
Somewhere far away the Severn presses,
alert at flood-tide. And everywhere rhythms
are turning their little gold cogs, caught
in her waterfalling energy.

# PLUMS

When their time comes they fall
without wind, without rain.
They seep through the trees' muslin
in a slow fermentation.

Daily the low sun warms them
in a late love that is sweeter
than summer. In bed at night
we hear heartbeat of fruitfall.

The secretive slugs crawl home
to the burst honeys, are found
in the morning mouth on mouth,
inseparable.

We spread patchwork counterpanes
for a clean catch. Baskets fill,
never before such harvest,
such a hunters' moon burning

the hawthorns, drunk on syrups
that are richer by night
when spiders are pitching
tents in the wet grass.

This morning the red sun
is opening like a rose
on our white wall, prints there
the fishbone shadow of a fern.

The early blackbirds fly
guilty from a dawn haul
of fallen fruit. We too
breakfast on sweetnesses.

Soon plum trees will be bone,
grown delicate with frost's
formalities. Their black
angles will tear the snow.


# MRS FROST

Turning my head a moment
from the geriatrics' ward
I see the bare wood bowed
quietly under the rain,
mists rising in silence.

Her white head is lowered
to her one good shaking hand,
clear thoughts rising from a body
ninety-two years old and done-for,
waiting to look up, blue, blind,

from another century
when I stop reading. Portia
perfectly remembered, just
and gentle in her mind and mine.
The undiscriminating rain

brisk as nurses, chills the wood
to the bone as night comes on.
In the beaded silks of rain
the trees feed secretly
while she, not sleeping, remembers.

## SHADOWS IN LLANBADARN

All shadows on the wall are blue.
Ladder-shadow. The rope askew
on the tenth rung. The Manx kitten
leaping the gap to the orchard wall.
Yours, searching the February soil
for points of green. Papery brown
flowers of dead hydrangeas stir.

From the wall to the tenth rung
the kitten drops and settles, fur
black and tiger-barred with black,
tense at the rope a breath scares.
In her face the sudden sticky green
of buds in darkness burns with sun.
Your shadow turns. I hear it on the stair.

The ladder's last. The falling sun
gradually drowns it, rung by rung.

# ANDREW WATERMAN

## THE SONG

She sang the song the Belgian refugees
brought to the valley's mills in the Great War.
Straight in his narrow chair her husband sat,
blending a phrase. They were young then.

Their young have gone away. When her eyes went
he sold the weaver's-cottage, brought her down
to the terrace in the Bottom, fixed downstairs
for her wheelchair: bedroom, bath, no doors.

He does the women's work, and washes her.
When relatives call she talks of the old view
from home up on the Edge — moor, clough and sky.
But massive today in a darkening brown room

she sings the strange French words the Belgians taught her,
as if the mind's lens pours all summers since
back on one blot of light. She was young then,
the foreign music was the outside world.

Charged with its resonance the flowered teaset
on the Welsh dresser is set vibrating:
speckless teapot, milk-jug, rows of cups
she kept for best, and never filled or drank from.

## THE TWO ROADS

The fork in the path
came up before
I was ready to choose;
I found I had taken
the sky road. At first
I could glimpse through thicket
the other lane dipping,
escorted by water,
between flowering banks,
rollered lawns, white stone dwellings.

A turn lost the view.
And what with the rain
closing in, the unsheltered
climbing a stony
road riding blown grass,
it was only attaining
the ridge I could look
down through snatches of cloud
at the coast road whole:
past meadows where cows
stood in clusters it followed
the strand to the bay's
bluest haven, a house,
sunlit garden, child playing
as if who belong there
might have been me;
who appearing now
did not look up,
would be deaf at such distance
to the nothing I knew
was all I could say now.


# FROM THE OTHER COUNTRY

But you do not consider how long I have lived in this country.
Its skies move through my skull, and the changing light
over the water; like whales the humped mountains
surface in my dreams, and never were trees
thwart like these in flight from the salt harsh gales.

The customs of the people, it is true,
are not mine; in farms and one-street towns
they enact strict rituals of thrift, worship, pleasure.
Lights burn late where slow accounts are reckoned,
the drunk crashes prone in dying embers,

and beneath tribal tokens, ancient recitations.
Often indeed through main street and glen
drums throb savage annunciation, the door
opens to a rain of bullets, car-lights pick out
the corpse in a ditch. 'It's a madness going on,'

they say. Did you think madness so dull?
Look: how finite among the weltering green
these settlements, no margins to nourish the odd.
Knowing their place, they grow, pray, wed, kill, die.
Even their knowing smiles have a terrible innocence

which you do not understand. Nor, though you hear,
how their soft gutturals and singing intonation
infect my accent. I am welcomed
in bars and corner-shops, with 'It's a soft night.'
And yes, I have loved their girls.

See, where fine white clouds drift high above the meadow
the small farm daydreams all doors open:
they are all gone round the bend of the field, out of change.
Behind the clock on the mantel dust thickens on letters
strangely–deciphered, from children 'across the water'.

From where, too, on my screen come shimmering
images of the old labyrinthine cities,
sanities. Which I can revisit, resume
undetected; noticing how they find
bestial or glamorous our banalities,

and do not see the detail beneath stark outlines.
I am no longer sure that I wish to return,
even though it is winter here now, the sky and land
seeping greyly together. Unsettled, defined
by difference, I find I can live with this,

am strangely involved in, call it, a climate.
Yes, as the mad wind rises, sets the sea
resonating, whips waves white, and plucks
tiles from thin roofs, above which gulls
weave lamentation's dissonant vocables.

# PLAYING THROUGH OLD GAMES OF CHESS

A crane-fly trembles in the windowpane
as it has since before there were windows . . .
I play through old games of chess: their rich diapason
a blossoming in the room, as of huge heavy-headed roses.

Outside, the hottest summer since records began,
and the traffic-lights signalling insane morse,
a jabber of red green amber, somewhere a computer
has overheated, fouling the traffic and tempers

are overheated, and all along the Thames
the bridges shove themselves over from metal expansion.
Ah, the ecologists say, it is carbon dioxide
irreversibly building up in the upper atmosphere

due to industrial waste, and all kinds of waste
accumulate irreversibly, and we record it,
even the mineral ores of language processed through
to a standing slag beyond recycling;

and economists say it is the economy overheated.
The plane trees shimmer through rising petrol fumes,
and children's voices ascend to tinkle against the bowl
of a blue sky hazed with entropy, our last heat-death.

I reset the pieces and start again:
Steinitz versus Tchigorin, Ruy Lopez, Morphy Defence,
Havana, 1892, and decorously
the opposite knights step forth, the kings are castled to safety

for a while. And still for a while
beyond the cities in meadows (but a hum of traffic hanging)
the cows, as then, stand four-square over their shadows,
while one by one white petals slip into sun-dappled water

to float, for a while; and the woods are dark with summer,
greenness sloping to greenness to a far
horizon marked with the faint stroke of a steeple
as it has been since before there were

— steeples, I almost said. At least as when
all history seemed a sort of sunlit incline upwards,
with problems like the Balkans, abolishing cholera, crime,
certainly soluble, and change meant improvement,

hygiene, gas cooking, fast travel, the bioscope.
Beneath 'Truman, Hanbury, Buxton & Comps. Entire'
the old photograph shows clay pipes and boaters around an
    ale-bench,
and Spoonbeam is not out at lunch for Lancs for ever,

while at dusk, his cycle-lamp catching gold motes
along deep lanes where roots twist and convolvulus clings,
comes Cholmondeley to talk, over whiskey by leaded windows,
of *The Origin of Species* or *The Idylls of the King*.

The pawn-structure looks sound, across the board *andante*
the full orchestration unfolds, with recurring motifs and
    grace-notes,
rounding Good Hope the *Ariel* bringing home tea from China,
cablegrams under the sea, while in Afghan hill-posts

or where a delta's archipelagos of bamboo huts
coalesce to a port of old palaces, crumbling pagodas,
men with iron moustaches bat out their time
outstaring all sundowns from the verandah.

Of course, through the looking-glass all was different,
and moving forward got you nowhere, the miners
stonily piling their barrows after the latest eviction
cannot see their great-grandsons' Cortinas, package-tour fritterings,

and the husband who tendered with flowers the most honourable
    intentions
is hanging his stovepipe hat on the bedposts of whores;
and every life dark-edged, the hushed death-rooms, the infant
    graves,
and perhaps it is all the tinman's dream

who stationed at the street corner pedals his grinding-wheel
for ever. And as for the countless hordes
of Indian and Chinese, it is not their game
at all, they have nothing to learn but patience.

Exchange of queens: the general liquidation
which follows seems to favour white, a sacrificial
manoeuvre clinches things, for a while. If today
in Flanders the farmer again wades through barley where all nature

was murdered, still the old dynasts have toppled like chess-kings,
and however we go through the motions again
(the squares are being done up, houses wormy with their past
are scoured, the cellars blocked off as if there were bones down in
    them,

layers of cheap flowered paper torn from each wall),
or trace the lines not followed, unrealised combinations
in notes as much as the moves played part of the game,
the quality of that long, lost summer cannot be restored

— when June rang like a gong for Pax Britannica,
and Europe's chordage held the world enthralled;
and in London, St. Petersburg, Vienna or Baden Baden
the old chess-masters' arias thrilled. Until Lasker, who

would research Relativity, talk with Einstein, flee
the Nazis, shifted a piece irrevocably changing
the chemistry of the game, its lovely architectonics;
while a crane-fly trembled in the windowpane.


# AT THE SEA'S EDGE

This sea like shot-silk, every day such light
gilding my window-frames. I drowse, afloat
in summer; and some sound I have always known,
say that lawnmower's gritty whirring, makes believe
there are continuities woven through the years.
Even that mad-looking spiky hasp of a thing
that palpitates on my pane, I have known before,

fastening to me one childhood evening when
I sifted through my coin-collection, francs,
marks, annas, coins with squiggles, blackening
silver threepennies, and the massy copper
George III penny, perhaps then the last time
dropping back in the soft bag, me not realising.
So many things put by for the last time!

Or lost. All that was meant. As when, sun gilding
our handlebars I cycled out with Pam
whose back to touch was velvet. Who is she now,
with daughters maybe older than us then?
Well, but we got beyond Coulsdon anyhow,
stood mazed in hot fields tasting ears of wheat
under blue vacancy empty as today's.

Some purposes are approximated, reached
provisionally, as day floats into day
each what we point ourselves from, promising,
no place to linger, but for drinks and chat,
brief sexual crestings. 'But what next?' we say,
and then distracted perhaps only because
of chance conjunction: girl, sun, bluebell–wood.

The expense of spirit for so much betrayed!
I founder into it; until again
the lawnmower chirring, insect on the pane
steady me, beachcombing what swims up,
flotsam, precipitates not all beautiful,
but hard; this ring kept, which the world whatever
it's coming to no longer has a use for.

One wants things should mean something overall,
at least be shaped from one act somewhere back
— as picking a single flower can ramify
past sight to huge loves or unblossomings.
But that dog trotting by now with wrapped meat
as such dogs always have, connects with no
last pattern, is familiar to deceive,

and the sea refulgent with a creamy light
where tiny crestings randomly repeat,
pure freedom merely; plunge in off the strand
and feel its coldness. I have heard it cry
all night upon those outflung arms of coast
— soaring fluencies of line perfecting
motion to far paradigms of peace.

# BUNHILL FIELDS

Crammed, blackening, subsiding, warped,
some weathered past deciphering,
dissenters' gravestones; railed off from
what's smoothed to lawn and flowerbeds,

where pensioners put out to grass
and girls with limpid eyes and prams
sun through the weekday afternoon,
as Milton, blind nearby, once did.

The risen City overlooks
here Cromwells, Wesleys, and the bones
of Bunyan, Blake, Defoe. Above
and underneath the grass now, stillness.

Broken by what taps my cheek
flaked from the opulence of trees
repeating autumn's fall of life
to headstone, greensward, marking time.

## *from* OUT FOR THE ELEMENTS

'So anyway, I've taken a scunner
to the whole scene entirely. Not
much future being a rear-gunner
in a Belfast milkfloat. I've got
sick sore tired of it altogether,
of all sides' bigotry, and whether
our Provies fighting with our Sticks
does anything for Catholics
I'd question. And so, should I rather
have kept thick with the girls who pour
at shift-ends out of Gallaghers or
the dinghy-factory, in a lather
of "How's-about-yous?" clicking bags
arm-in-arm as they hoke for fags?'

From Belfast now, where like a flame on
ruins a wild vitality
dances — whoever you'd lay blame on
for all destroyed, deformity
of spirit, craven adorations —
west and south by slow gradations
modulating, Ireland yields
itself: white stone farms pegging fields
that fire with whin each May, cool rivers
winding through alder, green townlands
tricked out each Twelfth with flags and bands
and Orange arches; country-livers,
marketing in slow one-street towns;
byres where the searching soldier frowns.

Jaguars parked on mud outside the
disco-lounges of shore hotels
(each weekend's hangover must ride the
sabbatical tumult of bells);
fishermen out on Lough Neagh steering
frail boats; tenebrous packed bars hearing
'Carrickfergus', 'Mna na h Eireann',
on uilleann pipes, flute and bodhran.
Night over all, a full moon bowling
among cloud-slipstream glitters from
pooled water and that milk-churn bomb
triggered for Ferret-cars patrolling
the border lanes, lads homesick for
city-lights far from this mad war.

Each morning, Radio Ulster's prattle
about it all, as bread vans drive
past hedge and sheugh and mist-wreathed cattle
('Three dead, one serious but alive')
delivering nourishment to rural
estates and lonely farms. A plural
half-listening regret's expressed,
'Surely, it's dreadful. Sean, get dressed
or it's the school bus you'll be losing,'
lost among purpled peaks and slopes
where high springs generate like hopes
gushing what falters downhill, oozing
to loughs where Ireland in chaste dress
kneels to its mirrored loveliness.

This land's reflective waters chilling
wind-humoured reeds, its purities
of line and colour, huge skies filling
with such mutating mysteries
of light, clouds massing and dispersing,
the mountains shrugging on rehearsing
tonal varieties of green
to the last essence, whether seen
through sun or raindrifts all compelling
love by sublimity more sheer
than what's botched, tamed, in England's mere
sad patchwork, so our spoiled lives dwelling
among it crave its blessing, still
neglects to answer; never will.

And west, and never mind the border,
past Muckish, Maam Cross, Ballina,
to Europe's wildest fringe, an order
of being *in extremis*: far
white cottages with turfstacks scattered
along some quartzveined glen-side battered
by gales, where barefoot children herd
cattle along mired lanes; absurd
beauty soars all around, descends to
ribboning miles of golden strand.
No data — slums, boutiques, smart brand-
names, aerosoled slogans, décor trends — to
help social scientists who'd confine
life to roles Kew or Bow define.

Two tinker kids with switches bowling
a tyre down a remote bohereen,
the backcloth mountains, and sheep strolling
among dead sheep's bones: I have seen
wildernesses of greenness barely
netted by drystone walls, one squarely
imperturbable Norman tower
perhaps by water; with each shower
bounty of rainbows arched on passes
where windswept wayside shrines gleam or
some tumbled cabin, roof and door
jaggedly gaping. Over grasses
in derelict graveyards by the sea
light blows in waves, swarms each bent tree.

Crying on cliffs, the western ocean
utters itself to fishermen
intimate with its ficklest motion,
trusting in what they have to when
the tide allows: in Cleggan, Downings,
Cahirciveen, families with drownings
throughout their ancestries like knots
in sea-wrack. That horizon's what's
lured since the early hermits shivered
in loose stone chapels on bare fangs
of rock where the Atlantic bangs,
their skulls blown clean till vision quivered
alive on solitude, stars, night,
conjuring ecstasies of light.

# A WINTER'S TALE

Woodpigeons brooding in a sunlit glade.
From the hollow-rooted tree by the green pond
sudden to glimpse a dragonfly's blue blade
glitter then gone; day-dreams and water-sound;

and 'such a day tomorrow as today,
and to be boy eternal'. Other weather
tobogganing-time, sharp autumn, foaming may,
varying, drew rich pattern's threads together.

Like stories whose *And then?* . . . *And then?* . . . returned
to *Safe home round the fireside* . . . Where, December
mashing lawn past the glass as when I learned
of light-years-distant nebulae, I remember

how feeling inside so much so far and bright,
clockwork-routine in long continuance,
seemed confirmation then, like bed each night,
not solitude terrorised by wastes of chance.

So what changed? Rather, how? Yes, adolescence
tuning the world out of itself, and no
hint of idealism's corrosive essence.
But more, it's realising life's cyclic show

cherishes only foliage, not leaf.
Still this drab winter's ceremonious.
Though eyes too young to know the vision brief
don't need estrangement's words to gloss it thus.

# DEREK MAHON

## THE FORGER

When I sold my fake Vermeers to Goering
Nobody knew, nobody guessed
The agony, the fanaticism
Of working beyond criticism
And better than the best.

When they hauled me before the war-crimes tribunal
No one suspected, nobody knew
The agony of regrets
With which I told my secrets.
They missed the point, of course —
To hell with the national heritage,
I sold my *soul* for potage.

The experts were good value, though,
When they went to work on my studio —
Not I, but *they* were the frauds.
I revolutionized their methods.

Now, nothing but claptrap
About 'mere technique' and 'true vision',
As if there were a distinction —
Their way of playing it down.
But my genius will live on;
For even at one remove
The thing I meant was love.

And I too have wandered
In the dark streets of Holland
With hunger at my belly
When the mists rolled in from the sea;
And I too have suffered
Obscurity and derision,
And sheltered in my heart of hearts
A light to transform the world.

# AN IMAGE FROM BECKETT
*for Doreen Douglas*

In that instant
There was a sea, far off,
As bright as lettuce,

A northern landscape
And a huddle
Of houses along the shore.

Also, I think, a white
Flicker of gulls
And washing hung to dry —

The poignancy of those
Back-yards – and the gravedigger
Putting aside his forceps.

Then the hard boards
And darkness once again.
But in that instant

I was struck
By the sweetness and light,
The sweetness and light,

Imagining what grave
Cities, what lasting monuments,
Given the time.

They will have buried
My great-grandchildren, and theirs,
Beside me by now

With a subliminal batsqueak
Of reflex lamentation.
Our hair and excrement

Litter the rich earth,
Changing, second by second,
To civilizations.

It was good while it lasted,
And if it only lasted
The biblical span

Required to drop six feet
Through a glitter of wintry light,
There is No one to blame.

Still, I am haunted
By that landscape,
The soft rush of its winds,

The uprightness of its
Utilities and schoolchildren —
To whom in my will,

This, I have left my will.
I hope they had time,
And light enough, to read it.


# CONSOLATIONS OF PHILOSOPHY

When we start breaking up in the wet darkness
And the rotten boards fall from us, and the ribs
Crack under the constriction of tree roots
And the seasons slip from the fields unknown to us,

Oh, then there will be the querulous complaining
From citizens who had never dreamt of this —
Who, shaken to the bone in their stout boxes
By the latest bright cars, will not inspect them

And, kept awake by the tremors of new building,
Will not be there to comment. When the broken
Wreath bowls are speckled with rain-water
And the grass grows wild for want of a caretaker,

There will be time to live through in the mind
The lives we might have led, and get them right;
To lie in silence listening to the wind
Call for the living through the livelong night.

# DOG DAYS

'When you stop to consider
The days spent dreaming of a future
And say then, that was my life.'

For the days are long —
From the first milk van
To the last shout in the night,
An eternity. But the weeks go by
Like birds; and the years, the years
Fly past anti-clockwise
Like clock hands in a bar mirror.


# THE SNOW PARTY
*for Louis Asekoff*

Bashō, coming
To the city of Nagoya,
Is asked to a snow party.

There is a tinkling of china
And tea into china;
There are introductions.

Then everyone
Crowds to the window
To watch the falling snow.

Snow is falling on Nagoya
And farther south
On the tiles of Kyōto.

Eastward, beyond Irago,
It is falling
Like leaves on the cold sea.

Elsewhere they are burning
Witches and heretics
In the boiling squares,

Thousands have died since dawn
In the service
Of barbarous kings;

But there is silence
In the houses of Nagoya
And the hills of Ise.


# A DISUSED SHED IN CO. WEXFORD

*Let them not forget us, the weak souls among the asphodels.*
— Seferis, *Mythistorema*

*for J. G. Farrell*

Even now there are places where a thought might grow —
Peruvian mines, worked out and abandoned
To a slow clock of condensation,
An echo trapped for ever, and a flutter
Of wildflowers in the lift-shaft,
Indian compounds where the wind dances
And a door bangs with diminished confidence,
Lime crevices behind rippling rainbarrels,
Dog corners for bone burials;
And in a disused shed in Co. Wexford,

Deep in the grounds of a burnt-out hotel,
Among the bathtubs and the washbasins
A thousand mushrooms crowd to a keyhole.
This is the one star in their firmament
Or frames a star within a star.
What should they do there but desire?
So many days beyond the rhododendrons
With the world waltzing in its bowl of cloud,
They have learnt patience and silence
Listening to the rooks querulous in the high wood.

They have been waiting for us in a foetor
Of vegetable sweat since civil war days,
Since the gravel-crunching, interminable departure
Of the expropriated mycologist.
He never came back, and light since then

Is a keyhole rusting gently after rain.
Spiders have spun, flies dusted to mildew
And once a day, perhaps, they have heard something —
A trickle of masonry, a shout from the blue
Or a lorry changing gear at the end of the lane.

There have been deaths, the pale flesh flaking
Into the earth that nourished it;
And nightmares, born of these and the grim
Dominion of stale air and rank moisture.
Those nearest the door grow strong —
'Elbow room! Elbow room!'
The rest, dim in a twilight of crumbling
Utensils and broken flower-pots, groaning
For their deliverance, have been so long
Expectant that there is left only the posture.

A half century, without visitors, in the dark —
Poor preparation for the cracking lock
And creak of hinges. Magi, moonmen,
Powdery prisoners of the old regime,
Web-throated, stalked like triffids, racked by drought
And insomnia, only the ghost of a scream
At the flash-bulb firing squad we wake them with
Shows there is life yet in their feverish forms.
Grown beyond nature now, soft food for worms,
They lift frail heads in gravity and good faith.

They are begging us, you see, in their wordless way,
To do something, to speak on their behalf
Or at least not to close the door again.
Lost people of Treblinka and Pompeii!
'Save us, save us,' they seem to say,
'Let the god not abandon us
Who have come so far in darkness and in pain.
We too had our lives to live.
You with your light meter and relaxed itinerary,
Let not our naive labours have been in vain!'

# THE RETURN
*for John Hewitt*

I am saying goodbye to the trees,
The beech, the cedar, the elm,
The mild woods of these parts
Misted with car exhaust,
And sawdust, and the last
Gasps of the poisoned nymphs.

I have watched girls walking
And children playing under
Lilac and rhododendron,
And me flicking my ash
Into the rose bushes
As if I owned the place;

As if the trees responded
To my ignorant admiration
Before dawn when the branches
Glitter at first light,
Or later on when the finches
Disappear for the night;

And often thought if I lived
Long enough in this house
I would turn into a tree
Like somebody in Ovid
— A small tree certainly
But a tree nonetheless —

Perhaps befriend the oak,
The chestnut and the yew,
Become a home for birds,
A shelter for the nymphs,
And gaze out over the downs
As if I belonged here too.

But where I am going the trees
Are few and far between.
No richly forested slopes,
Not for a long time,
And few winking woodlands;
There are no nymphs to be seen.

Out there you would look in vain
For a rose bush; but find,
Rooted in stony ground,
A last stubborn growth
Battered by constant rain
And twisted by the sea-wind

With nothing to recommend it
But its harsh tenacity
Between the blinding windows
And the forests of the sea,
As if its very existence
Were a reason to continue.

Crone, crow, scarecrow,
Its worn fingers scrabbling
At a torn sky, it stands
On the edge of everything
Like a burnt-out angel
Raising petitionary hands.

Grotesque by day, at twilight
An almost tragic figure
Of anguish and despair,
It merges into the funeral
Cloud-continent of night
As if it belongs there.

*Lingfield-Coleraine, 1977*


# COURTYARDS IN DELFT
## —PIETER DE HOOCH, 1659
*for Gordon Woods*

Oblique light on the trite, on brick and tile —
Immaculate masonry, and everywhere that
Water tap, that broom and wooden pail
To keep it so. House-proud, the wives
Of artisans pursue their thrifty lives
Among scrubbed yards, modest but adequate.
Foliage is sparse, and clings. No breeze
Ruffles the trim composure of those trees.

No spinet-playing emblematic of
The harmonies and disharmonies of love;
No lewd fish, no fruit, no wide-eyed bird
About to fly its cage while a virgin
Listens to her seducer, mars the chaste
Precision of the thing and the thing made.
Nothing is random, nothing goes to waste:
We miss the dirty dog, the fiery gin.

That girl with her back to us who waits
For her man to come home for his tea
Will wait till the paint disintegrates
And ruined dykes admit the esurient sea;
Yet this is life too, and the cracked
Out-house door a verifiable fact
As vividly mnemonic as the sunlit
Railings that front the houses opposite.

I lived there as a boy and know the coal
Glittering in its shed, late-afternoon
Lambency informing the deal table,
The ceiling cradled in a radiant spoon.
I must be lying low in a room there,
A strange child with a taste for verse,
While my hard-nosed companions dream of war
On parched veldt and fields of rain-swept gorse;

For the pale light of that provincial town
Will spread itself, like ink or oil,
Over the not yet accurate linen
Map of the world which occupies one wall
And punish nature in the name of God.
If only, now, the Maenads, as of right,
Came smashing crockery, with fire and sword,
We could sleep easier in our beds at night.

# NORTH WIND: PORTRUSH

I shall never forget the wind
On this benighted coast.
It works itself into the mind
Like the high keen of a lost
Lear-spirit in agony
Condemned for eternity

To wander cliff and cove
Without comfort, without love.
It whistles off the stars
And the existential, black
Face of the cosmic dark:
We crouch to roaring fires.

Yet there are mornings when,
Even in midwinter, sunlight
Flares, and a rare stillness
Lies upon roof and garden,
Each object eldritch-bright,
The sea scarred but at peace.

Then, from the ship we say
Is the lit town where we live
(Our whiskey-and-forecast world),
A smaller ship that sheltered
All night in the restless bay
Will weigh anchor and leave.

What did they think of us
During their brief sojourn?
A string of lights on the prom
Dancing mad in the storm —
Who lives in such a place?
And will they ever return?

But the shops open at nine
As they have always done,
The wrapped-up bourgeoisie
Hardened by wind and sea.
The newspapers are late
But the milk shines in its crate.

Everything swept so clean
By tempest, wind and rain!
Elated, you might believe
That this was the first day —
A false sense of reprieve,
For the climate is here to stay.

So best prepare for the worst
That chaos and old night

Can do to us. Were we not
Raised on such expectations,
Our hearts starred with frost
Through countless generations?

Elsewhere the olive grove,
*Le déjeuner sur l'herbe,*
Poppies and parasols,
Blue skies and mythic love.
Here only the stricken souls
No spring can unperturb.

Prospero and his people never
Came to these stormy parts:
Few do who have the choice.
Yes, blasting the subtler arts,
That weird, plaintive voice
Choirs now and for ever.


# THE ANDEAN FLUTE

He dances to that music in the wood
As if history were no more than a dream.
Who said the banished gods were gone for good?

The furious rhythm creates a manic mood,
Piercing the twilight like a mountain stream.
He dances to that music in the wood.

We might have put on Bach or Buxtehude,
But a chance impulse chose the primal scream.
Who said the banished gods were gone for good?

An Inca frenzy fires his northern blood.
His child-heart picking up the tribal beam,
He dances to that music in the wood.

A puff of snow bursts where the birches brood;
Along the lane the earliest snowdrops gleam.
Who said the banished gods were gone for good?

It is the ancient cry for warmth and food
That moves him. Acting out an ancient theme,
He dances to that music in the wood.
Who said the banished gods were gone for good?


# TRACTATUS
*for Aidan Higgins*

'The world is everything that is the case'
From the fly giving up in the coal-shed
To the Winged Victory of Samothrace.
Give blame, praise, to the fumbling God
Who hides, shame-facèdly, His agèd face;
Whose light retires behind its veil of cloud.

The world, though, is also so much more —
Everything that is the case imaginatively.
Tacitus believed mariners could *hear*
The sun sinking into the western sea;
And who would question that titanic roar,
The steam rising wherever the edge may be?


# THE WOODS

Two years we spent
down there, in a quaint
outbuilding bright with recent paint.

A green retreat,
secluded and sedate,
part of a once great estate,

it watched our old
bone-shaker as it growled
with guests and groceries through heat and cold,

and heard you tocsin
meal-times with a spoon
while I sat working in the sun.

Above the yard
an old clock had expired
the night Lenin arrived in Petrograd.

Bourbons and Romanovs
had removed their gloves
in the drawing-rooms and alcoves

of the manor house;
but these illustrious
ghosts never imposed on us.

Enough that the pond
steamed, the apples ripened,
the conkers on the gravel opened.

Ragwort and hemlock,
cinquefoil and ladysmock
throve in the shadows at the back;

beneath the trees
foxgloves and wood-anemones
looked up with tearful metamorphic eyes.

We woke the rooks
on narrow, winding walks
familiar from the story books,

or visited
a disused garden shed
where gas-masks from the war decayed;

and we knew peace
splintering the thin ice
on the bath-tub drinking-trough for cows.

But how could we
survive indefinitely
so far from the city and the sea?

Finding, at last,
too creamy for our taste
the fat profusion of that feast,

we travelled on
to doubt and speculation,
our birthright and our proper portion.

Another light
than ours convenes the mute
attention of those woods tonight —

while we, released
from that pale paradise,
ponder the darkness in another place.

# JEREMY HOOKER

## LANDSCAPE OF THE DAYLIGHT MOON

I first saw it inland.
Suddenly, round white sides
Rose through the thin grass
And for an instant, in the heat,
It was dazzling; but afterwards
I thought mainly of darkness,
Imagining the relics of an original
Sea under the chalk, with fishes
Beneath the fields. Later,
Everywhere upon its surface
I saw the life of the dead;
Circle within circle of earthen
Shells, and in retraced curves
Like finger marks in pale sand,
The print of a primaeval lover.
Once, climbing a dusty track,
I found a sunshaped urchin,
With the sun's rays, white
With the dusts of the moon.
Fetish, flesh become stone,
I keep it near me. It is
A mouth on darkness, the one
Inexhaustible source of re-creation.

## PITTS DEEP

Over Abbey ploughland
On a brown, winter day
Of Cistercian calm,
No one will go observing
The silver bell mouth of the sky,
Or cross the manorial path
Into oakwoods descending
Almost to the water —
Except, perhaps, two friends
With a bottle of cheap wine
Who walk in confessional mood

Where forest ponies also go,
Trampling soiled, silky weed
On mudbanks and quills
Of bleached salt-grass,
Sowing a trail of droppings
On the stilled shore.

# FROM A PILL-BOX ON THE SOLENT

On a day of ripped cloud,
Angled light, wind against tide,
I am tempted to begin
The story of my life.

Waves come from far off,
Through the gap they have made,
Between Purbeck and Wight.

Surf booms in the pill-box,
Rattles the shingle,
Folds over it, unfolds,
Laying it bare.

Let it blow sand or salt.
Here at least I tread without fear
Of unsettling dust.

# RICE GRASS
*(Spartina Townsendii)*

Praise one appearing
lowly, no man's rose,
but with roots far-reaching
out and down.

Give homage to a spartan cross,
native and American,
hardier and more adaptable
than those; nearly a newcomer
but one that, by staying put
has made itself a home;
also a traveller east and west.

Celebrate the entertainer
of sea aster, sea lavender,
thrift and nesting gulls;
lover of mud and salt;
commoner and useful colonist,
converter from ooze
of land where a foot may fall.

## SOFT DAYS AFTER SNOW

Soft days after snow,
    snowdrops
under sycamores beside the stream,
earth brown and crumbling.

Now the dark gleams softly
under catkins and water below,
alight in the February sun.
And I who desired
    eyes washed clean
as melting snow,
radiant at the point of fall,
know that every word obscures
the one I want to know.

Now soft days bear us
who take each other's hands,
and on their surface
    colder than blood
our brief appearances.

Though snowdrops follow the snow,
    and the water burns,
darkness carries them.

Our faces are taken away.

Where do you go,
    unspeakable love?

# ON SAINT DAVID'S DAY

For Dewi Sant, an eye
of yellow in the daffodils,
the curlew from the sea,
the hare that lollops by a gate
   which opens wide
on far Plynlimmon,
Cader Idris
and the airy rockface
   of the northern sky.

I too would name
a tribute of these things:
cold wind,
white sun of March,
   the boundaries
whose handywork of stone
shines through the falling earth.

I turn towards the mynydd
in a film of light,
   and turning
ask of Dewi Sant
   his benediction
on these words that settle
where the uplands rise.

# BRYNBEIDOG

For ten years the sycamores
have turned about us, the Beidog
has run with leaves, and ice and sun.
I have turned the earth, thrown up
blue chip and horseshoe; from near fields
sheep and bullocks have looked in.

We have shared weathers
with the stone house; kept its silence;
listened under winds lifting slates
for a child's cry; all we have
the given space has shaped, pointing
our lights seen far off

as a spark among the scattered sparks.
  The mountain above
has been rock to my drifting mind.

Where all is familiar, around us
the country with it language
gives all things other names;
there is darkness on bright days
and on the stillest a wind
that will not let us settle,
but blows the dust from loved
things not possessed or known.

## WIND BLEW ONCE

Wind blew once till it seemed
the earth would be skinned from the fields,
the hard roots bared.
  Then it was again
a quiet October,
red berries on grey rock
and blue sky, with a buzzard crying.

I scythed half-moons in long grass,
with nettle-burn stinging my arms,
bringing the blood's rhythm back.
  At night
in our room we lay in an angle
between two streams,
with sounds of water meeting,
  and by day
the roads ran farther,
joined and formed a pattern
at the edge of vast, cloudy hills.

  The house was small
against the mountain; from above,
a stone on a steep broad step
of falling fields; but around us
the walls formed a deep channel,
with marks of other lives, holding
its way from worked moorland
to this Autumn with an open sky.

# BEHIND THE LIGHTS

Last night, I looked from the Island.
   Then I was again
behind the lights, living there
blindly, where the mainland
long shore shone, with breaks
at Forest and river mouths,
a ghostly smoke round chimneys;
till suddenly, a green light
on black water cut across my view.

Tonight, I return
to another darkness, the house
strangely cold, behind me
the long road back to Wales.
It will be dark in an hour
but now the sun setting
picks out a fox in the field
above the house, cutting across my view.
There he goes gingerly,
a lordly fox, golden red.
   Tired, I see
a green light on black water.
Better to follow the fox,
from sunlight into shadow,
on his cold way home.

# DRAGONS IN THE SNOW

Thaw to the hedgerows
left white crosses on the hill,
   the first thrush sang.

Now a buzzard cries, confirming
   silence under all.

The few bare trees are darker
for the fall that covers
   boundaries,
and in their place reveals
contrasting absolutes.

We are so small,
the boy and I, between
the snowclouds and the snow.

He starts from here,
who talks of dragons
as we walk, the first today
to leave a human sign
beside the marks of sheep and crow.

He warms me
with confiding hand
and fiery talk,
    who also start
upon the ground
of choice, the silence
answering the choice;
happy to be small, and walk,
and hear of dragons in the snow.

# JEFFREY WAINWRIGHT

## THOMAS MÜNTZER
*for David Spooner*

Thomas Müntzer was a Protestant reformer in the early years of the German Reformation. He was a radical and a visionary both in theology and politics for whom religious thought and experience became integrated with ideas and movements towards social revolution.

Travelling through Germany, preaching and writing, continually in trouble with the authorities, he came to support and lead struggles by common people against the monopolies of wealth and learning. In 1525, in the Peasant War, he led an army against the princes which was heavily defeated at Frankenhausen. Müntzer was subsequently captured and executed.

> *Doubt is the Water, the movement to good and evil.*
> *Who swims on the water without a saviour is between*
> *life and death.* —Müntzer

> *I have seen in my solitude*
> *very clear things*
> *that are not true.* —Machado

I

Just above where my house sits on the slope
Is a pond, a lodge when the mine was here,
Now motionless, secretive, hung in weeds.

Sometimes on clear nights I spread my arms wide
And can fly, stiff but perfect, down
Over this pond just an inch above the surface.

When I land I have just one, two drops of water
On my beard. I am surprised how quick
I have become a flier, a walker on air.

II

I see my brother crawling in the woods
To gather snails' shells. *This is not*
*A vision.* Look carefully and you can tell

How he is caught in the roots of a tree
Whose long branches spread upwards bearing as
Fruit gardeners and journeymen, merchants

And lawyers, jewellers and bishops,
Cardinals chamberlains nobles princes
Branch by branch kings pope and emperor.

III

I feel the very earth is against me.
Night after night she turns in my sleep
And litters my fields with stones.

I lie out all summer spread like a coat
Over the earth one night after another
Waiting to catch her. And then

She is mine and the rowan blooms —
His black roots swim out and dive to subdue her —
His red blood cracks in the air and saves me.

IV

How many days did I search in my books
For such power, crouched like a bird under
My roof and lost to the world?

Scholars say God no longer speaks with us
Men — as though he has grown dumb, lost his tongue,
(Cut out for stealing a hare or a fish?)

Now I explode — out of this narrow house,
My mind lips hands skin my whole body
Cursing them for their flesh and their learning —

V

*dran dran dran* we have the sword — the purity
Of metal — the beauty of blood falling.
Spilt it is refreshed, it freshens also

The soil which when we turn it will become
Paradise for us once rid of these maggots
And their blind issue. They will seek about

And beg you: 'Why is this happening to us?
Forgive us Forgive us', pleading now for
*Mercy* a new sweet thing they've found a taste for.

VI

So you see from this how I am — Müntzer:
'O bloodthirsty man' breathing not air
But fire and slaughter, a true phantasist —

'A man born for heresy and schism',
'This most lying of men', 'a mad dog'.
And all because I speak and say: God made

All men free with His own blood shed.
Hold everything in common. Share evil.
And I find I am a god, like all men.

VII

He teaches the gardener from his trees
And the fisherman from his catch, even
The goldsmith from the testing of his gold.

In the pond the cold thick water clothes me.
I live with the timorous snipe, beetles
And skaters, the pike smiles and moves with me.

We hold it in common without jealousy.
Touch your own work and the simple world.
In these unread creatures sings the real gospel.

VIII

I have two guilders for a whole winter.
I ask for company and food from beggars,
The very poorest, those I fancy most

Blessed . . . I am in love with a girl
And dare not tell her so . . she makes me
Like a boy again — sick and dry-mouthed.

How often have I told you God comes only
In your apparent abandonment. This is
The misery of my exile — I was elected to it.

## IX

My son will not sleep. The noise
And every moving part of the world
Shuttles round him, making him regard it,

Giving him — only four years old! — no peace.
He moves quietly in his own purposes
Yet stays joyless. There is no joy to be had,

And he knows that and is resigned to it.
At his baptism we dressed him in white
And gave him salt as a symbol of this wisdom.

## X

I am white and broken. I can hardly gasp out
What I want to say, which is: *I believe in God* . . .
At Frankenhausen His promised rainbow

Did bloom in the sky, silky and so bold
No one could mistake it. Seeing it there
I thought I could catch their bullets in my hands.

An article of faith. I was found in bed
And carried here for friendly
Interrogation. They ask me *what I believe*.

## XI

Their horsemen ride over our crops kicking
The roots from the ground. They poison wells
And throw fire down the holes where people hide.

An old woman crawls out. She is bleeding
And screaming so now they say they are sorry
And would like to bandage her. She won't

Go with them. She struggles free. *I see it
I see it* — she is bound to die . . .
This is the glittering night we wake in.

## XII

I lie here for a few hours yet, clothed still
In my external life, flesh I have tried
To render pure, and a scaffold of bones.

I would resign all interest in it.
To have any love for my own fingered
Body and brain is a luxury.

History, which is Eternal Life, is what
We need to celebrate. Stately tearful
Progress . . . you've seen how I have wept for it.


# SENTIMENTAL EDUCATION

*Delicatesse*

Word of this 'revolution' drifts to us.
I sit, smoke, pore over papers
For the experts' views — though you distract me.
One can conjure whole suburbs, postmen,
Plumbers, flushed inelegant shopgirls
Ardent to be tearing up cobble stones.

What is all that compared with an eel stew,
Chicken, hard bread, and wine sharp on the tongue?
We eat ravenously, honest jagged knives
In our hands, the light of candles
Surrendering to your eyes. Ah my sweet,
To lose you will be such delicious sorrow!


*The Ruin'd Abbey*

A thousand years ago, the monks hereabouts
Would recognize early promise. There were
Openings for the right humility,
The sound contribution to scholarship.
Founded on such rock, juggler or jongleur,
There was no need to play with words.

I see you are not interested.
But where you sit to take off your shoes
Are tiles beautifully engraved with the Serpent
And the Fruit. Aware as I am of my own
Glibnesses, repetitions, minor faults, it is
A theme I never cease to contemplate.

*The Forest of Fontainebleau*

We admire the woodmen standing as we pass.
They sulk handsomely from the shoulders
Like beasts of the dark trees, wary of us.
One of them moves forward, and from a box,
Deliberately, staring straight into our eyes,
Produces three adders posed in his hands.

God knows it I am with you! all your trials
And your vexations and how you weigh them here
Bear upon me. But these your lithe spokesmen are
Too salutary, too quick. Show them to
Students, the educated poor, and tourists
Looking for something to amuse their friends.

# THE MAD TALK OF GEORGE III
# *and* A HYMN TO LIBERTY

> '. . . A century that thinks about liberation
> and phantasises prisons . . .'
> *Hans Magnus Enzensberger*

I

The slow-worm from my orchard seeking me
Creeps to my counterpane and waits,
His body curled here in my linened hands.
I lift him up and wind him round
My temples like a tender vine
Bringing his head to rise so neatly from my brow.
He is the slender vessel of my power,
My man of justice, not the stricken silver
Of a Pharaoh's crown but moving flesh,
And able to embrace us all.

## II

I sit alone in a chair on the bare moor,
The grass in flood in the orb I hold.
I sit as I did for anointment:
Attendants bringing up the coy canopy,
Archbishop Ambergris mounting the steps
To smooth my tousled head
For ministers to tell me their tales,
Doctors of the nerves, philosophers,
The black child of 'la liberté',
His eyes like scorched stones.


I sit alone in my chair on the bare moor,
Monarch of the yellow grass that laps my feet,
Of fearful space, a saucer of tussocks
And covert pools.
           I cannot abide wildness —
Satan is the prince of open air.
His will incites the mobile grass beyond itself
And hurls the tidy song-bird round the sky.
He it is brings, bemused from his club of devils,
The black child of 'la liberté' —
The blackened child of 'la liberté' —
For me to reason with.


Caught in the romance of king and child,
I show the boy this man,
Put up to hang,
Dreamed out of us and labouring in the air,
Who swims for a moment, rests,
Swims, and then rests.
The earth cannot hold his stillness.


## III

Candidus, my tall blood-prince, my grenadier,
Come with me since I love you.
Let us find a grove in middle Europe
Raised from sandy soil
Where the words will leave these stories

We have become and steal away,
Hallooing still one to another
Like accomplices on a dark road,
But gone.

> And we can dissolve,
blushes into white space    forgetting even
> the moss of a tree
> on its north side
the lost touch of it.


A HYMN TO LIBERTY

Count all the miner's hours, all his breathing
To the point of light.

A scud of air across the water's open face;
A child dabbles the flats of her palms
And laughs as she watches their play.
Each tree its silence breaks.

The movement of a breath of air across the lips
Creates the mind, and gives all of us our lives —

The inspired Republic,
A commune like the body with the air.

The child in love with the endless lake
Draws all her breath

# DAVID CONSTANTINE

## 'SOMEONE AT LEAST'

Someone at least reading about beauty in a room
Above the city has turned from the lamp once having heard
Her step behind him on the creaking board and until
Morning then and until, close in the eaves, birds woke
He was allowed to lie on the narrow bed with her
Under the maps that papered the sloped ceiling
Embracing her freely and planning with her journeys.


## THE DROWNED

Flat calm. The ships have gone.
By moonlight and by daylight one by one
Into a different world the drowned men rise
But cannot claw the sleep out of their eyes.
None such can know the bigger light from the less
Nor taste even the salt. Their heaviness
By no means may be leavened. Now they live
As timbers do where shipworms thrive
Only in what they feed. Strange things engross
The little galleries of thought after the loss
Of breath. The white clouds pass, but still
The drowned increase upon the senses till
The moon delivers them. On islands then
Seeing the lovely daylight watchful men
Come down and haul these burdens from the waves
And slowly cart them home and dig them graves.


## JOURNEY

Leaving the watered villages
The ash and poplar cool in their appearances
We came the companionable stream and I
To the last farm by and by.

For the whitethorn there
That was in flower later than anywhere
The girl water would not continue with me
I left her under the last tree.

Then some days following
I cast the long shadows of morning and evening
At noon I rode the sun on my shoulder
I was without water.

The white sheep lay
Like the remaining snow in February
On the north side of walls, in holes they hid
In poor embraces of shade.

Beyond pasture, beyond enclosure
On the common land of rock how far below were
Any cwm, any cradled pool and the water-veined
Wide folds. There intervened

No cloud, no bough between
Myself and the sun, only a hawk was shone
Steadily upon me in the grip of noon
I trod my shadow down.

I dreamed of the girl Artemis
She wore the ash and the poplar in a green dress
She led three burning hounds and seeing me
She smiled and set them free.


## 'FOR YEARS NOW'

For years now through your face the skull has shown
Nearer than through their living surface
The hills' bulk of dead stone;

And for years, watching you sleeping in that chair,
I have wished you might die with your face and hands composed,
Quietly sleeping there,

And trusted death to be so easy on you
That now one moment you would be sleeping and now
Have ceased without seeming to.

But today, watching you dead, I cannot think that there
Is any such slow passing into death from life
That the one might seem the other.

Finally the gap is absolute. Living
At all you were never nearly dead
And dead there is nothing

Vital of you in the abandoned face.
But the lack, the difference, has such nearness
We could almost embrace.

# 'YOU ARE DISTANT, YOU ARE ALREADY LEAVING'

You are distant, you are already leaving
You will have seemed here only between trains
And we are met here in the time of waiting
And what you last want is our eyes on you.

We shall have said nothing, we shall have done
Nothing in all that meantime there will
Have been not one gift pleasing us
You will have looked away and only behind
The pane of glass taking your seat with strangers
Being conveyed from here and when there is
No stay of parting you will smile perhaps
And give your face then the small mercy of weeping.

# WATCHING FOR DOLPHINS

In the summer months on every crossing to Piraeus
One noticed that certain passengers soon rose
From seats in the packed saloon and with serious
Looks and no acknowledgement of a common purpose
Passed forward through the small door into the bows
To watch for dolphins. One saw them lose

Every other wish. Even the lovers
Turned their desires on the sea, and a fat man

Hung with equipment to photograph the occasion
Stared like a saint, through sad bi-focals; others,
Hopeless themselves, looked to the children for they
Would see dolphins if anyone would. Day after day

Or on their last opportunity all gazed
Undecided whether a flat calm were favourable
Or a sea the sun and the wind between them raised
To a likeness of dolphins. Were gulls a sign, that fell
Screeching from the sky or over an unremarkable place
Sat in a silent school? Every face

After its character implored the sea.
All, unaccustomed, wanted epiphany,
Praying the sky would clang and the abused Aegean
Reverberate with cymbal, gong and drum.
We could not imagine more prayer, and had they then
On the waves, on the climax of our longing come

Smiling, snub-nosed, domed like satyrs, oh
We should have laughed and lifted the children up
Stranger to stranger, pointing how with a leap
They left their element, three or four times, centered
On grace, and heavily and warm re-entered,
Looping the keel. We should have felt them go

Further and further into the deep parts. But soon
We were among the great tankers, under their chains
In black water. We had not seen the dolphins
But woke, blinking. Eyes cast down
With no admission of disappointment the company
Dispersed and prepared to land in the city.


# LASITHI

Lasithi: notable for windmills. Summits are
    The petals of Lasithi and their snow
Streams underground. Ten thousand mills, sailing like toys,
    Crank it to surface into troughs. At dawn
The families come down to a lake of mist. Women
    In black unmoor and swivel the bare crosses
To feel the wind. The rods blossom and in its throat
    A well reaches for water like a man

Strangling. It mounts like birdsong then — o lovely work
    Of slowly scooping sails — it fills the reed,
The wells respire, the cisterns wait like mares and when
    In leaps, crashing like laughter, water comes,
A full wellbeing ascends and wets the walls and brims and
    Down the runnels like amusement overflows
Under the leaves, along the root-courses, and men
    Go about with hoes gently conducting it.

After the evaporation of the mist, under
    The sheer sun, under descending eagles,
Rimmed with snow, veined silvery with water and laced
    With childish flowers, the plateau works. The mills
Labour like lilies of the field, they toil and spin
    Like quivering cherry trees in one white orchard.


# 'THE TREES HERE . . .'

The trees here, though the wind leave off, never unbend.
Likewise when he sat the stick retained
The shape of the sixty years he had limped and leaned.
He would haul from under the bed with the crook-end

His bundle of photographs and the soldier's pay-book,
The usual service-medals and a card or two in silk.
The marriage bed was draped to the floor like a catafalque
And he hauled the War from under it. And when he spoke

Of the craters at Ypres he used the pool on Pool Green
As measure, and the island's entanglement of brambles when
He spoke of the wire. He rose, drinking gin,
Massive, straighter than his stick, and boys were shown

At the hoisting of his trouser up the sunless calf
A place that shrank like Lazarus from being raised,
A flesh the iron seemed only lately to have bruised.
And if one, being bidden and not in disbelief,

Put in the hand to prove him right who bet
That he was past hurt there — probing appalled
In that still weeping place the fingers rolled
Wondering between them an angle of iron grit.

For year by year his flesh, till he was dead,
Evicted its shrapnel, as the living ground
Puts out for the Parson or the Schoolmaster to find,
Scouring at leisure, another arrow head.

# ATLANTIS
*for Lotte and Hugh Shankland*

It dies hard, the notion of a just people;
    The wish that there should have been once mutual aid
Dies very hard. Through fire, through ghastly ash and any
    Smothering weight of water still we imagine
A life courteous and joyful; see them lightly clad
    Loving the sun, the vine and the grey olive.
Over the water, from trading, they come home winged
    With sails, their guide and harbinger the white dove.

I

The sea suddenly stood up vertical, sky-high,
Bristling with the planks of their peaceful ships.
The earth roared like a bull. They said Poseidon,
Breaker of lintels, was shaking them. There was fire too
Glaring like a red eye. But the unkindest
Was of all the four elements the purest
And to breathing man his being: the air
Clagged and precipitated in cankers of pumice
And thereafter for weeks in a fine dust.
Wherever the living air was welcome now
Ash entered and the hearts of houses ceased;
Their eyes, hurt by blows, were quite extinguished;
Their mouths, agape, were stopped. Ash filled
And softly embedded household pots, shrouded
Frescoes of air-breathing dolphins. Who survived
When the sun had wept and blinked its eyesight clear
Lame in the lungs saw only dust
Lying now quiet as snow. One inch of such —
That is from nail-end to the knuckle of the thumb —
Will render infertile the fruitful, the man-nurturing earth
For perhaps ten years. To them now kneeling on rock
Who had salted no fields, burned no olive groves
And poisoned nobody's wells, there remained no rod
To sound the ells, the fathoms, the generations of ash.

II

How deep below? None of the warring nations
Had length of chain to fathom at what depth
Atlantis lay. Nobody anchored there. But then —
In the days of death by impalement or the ganch
When Christian citizens of Candia ate
The besieging Turk — with a roar, witnesses say,
Like innumerable bulls, the sea, or the earth
Under the waters, rendered up to the surface
A new island, called nowadays *Kaimeni*,
The cinder. On Santorini the common people
Scratching a living in the old ash and pumice,
Remembered Kalliste and watched and prayed. But a scholar,
A believer in Atlantis, when the steam had thinned
Pulled out alone in a small boat. How great
Must have been his disappointment if he thought
Some glimmer of Atlantis might be vouchsafed him
(Who had done no especial wrong in wicked times)
If he hoped for some however dim intimation
Of their lost lovingkindness and wisdom: he saw
Only black smoking slag and ash, and smelled
An intimation of Christian Hell. Also
The hot sea soon uncaulked his punt and rowing
Desperately heavily for home he sank
In depths well known to be unfathomable.

# DICK DAVIS

## THE DIVER
*to Michaelis Nicoletséas*

The blue-cold spasm passes,
And he's broken in.
Assailed by silence he descends
Lost suddenly

To air and sunburned friends,
And wholly underwater now
He plies his strength against
The element that

Slows all probings to their feint.
Still down, till losing
Light he drifts to the wealthy wreck
And its shade-mariners

Who flit about a fractured deck
That holds old purposes
In darkness. He hesitates, then
Wreathes his body in.

## DIANA AND ACTAEON

He strays from sun to shade
And hears his favourite hound
Cry in some distant glade
That the tired deer is bayed.

At once, almost, the sound
Cannot be placed: he peers
Distractedly around
At unfamiliar ground.

The vagueness that he hears,
The eucalyptus trails,
Chafe at his nascent fears —
This way and that he veers,

Trapped, simple flesh: details
Half-lost between the trees
Cohere, and reason fails.
The goddess stoops, unveils —

Then naked stands, at ease,
Laved by the swirling stream:
Her hair stirs on the breeze,
And as he stares he sees

Her eyes fix his. They gleam
With infinite disdain.
His dogs' jaws snarl, but seem
Elsewhere — till through the dream

He feels the gash of pain.


## IRONY AND LOVE

Irony does not save:
The knowledge that you repeat
The infantile indiscreet
Reactions of the dead

Does not save. Irony
Says nothing when her hand
Gestures the promised land.
Irony is the dead

Who are not saved but see
Magnificent bold Orpheus
Claim the incredulous
Soon-to-return Eurydice.


## THE VIRGIN MARY

All these oppressed her:
                              light's
Peremptory pure glare
In summer, and the weak

Pallor of winter air;
Men's breath against her cheek,
And fruitless unshared nights.

Her strange clothes hung in mute
Annoying folds. She dreamed
Of splendour, undefined.
Naked, her body seemed
The useless withered rind
Of some prodigious fruit . . .

As if a distant call
Abstracted her, she bore
Her days indifferently,
And waited vaguely for
One slight contingency
That would resolve them all.


# TRAVELLING

1 *Pastoral*

Wild lavender and mint;
                            the mind's bemused
Sheep browse — cropping the serious anecdote,
Eschewing the dust of small-talk.
                                        Nearby,

Reason is a small boy who throws stones, sends
His yapping dog, to guide the errant flock.

2 *An Arrival*

Stranger, accept the little that is given —
The evening crowds, the quick unlooked-for smile
And the benediction of the sunset:
                                    who knows
But the tryst with the unknown god is here?

# DESERT STOP AT NOON

The house is one bare room
And only tea is served.
The old man, mild, reserved,
Shuffles into a gloom
Where mattresses are laid.
I sip, grateful for the cool shade.

His small son watches me,
Approaches, pertly smiles.
I know that thirty miles
Without a house or tree
Surround their crumbling shack.
I drink again, relax, smile back.

Water? and the boy's mother?
Both seem impossible —
Yet, here, my glass is full;
If I ask for another
The boy brings bitter tea
Then grins gap-toothed and begs from me.

And love? Impertinence
To ask. I could not grieve,
Born here, to have to leave:
But he, a man, years hence,
His life elsewhere, may weep
With need to see his father sleep

Again, as now he does,
In careless honesty —
Too old for courtesy —
Oblivious of us.
I pay, and leave the shade,
The dark recess these lives have made.

# MEMORIES OF COCHIN
*an epithalamium*

Through high defiles of warehouses that dwarf
With undetermined age the passer-by,
    We walk toward the ancient wharf,
Assailed by smells — sweet, pungent, bitter, dry:

The perfumed plunder of a continent.
To this shore Roman, Moslem, Christian, Jew
    Were gathered by the dense, sharp scent;
Absorbed now in the once-outlandish view

They camped by hills their children would call home.
So in the soil blurred Roman coins are found;
    Saint Thomas stepped into the foam
And strode ashore, and blessed the acrid ground;

Jews settled here when Sion was laid waste,
And Arabs edged tall dhows into the bay,
    Dutch burghers felt their northern haste,
Becalmed by slow siestas, ebb away . . .

So many faiths and peoples mingle here,
Breathing an air benign with spice and scent,
    That we, though strangers, should not fear
To invoke, in honour of our sacrament,

The sensual, wise genius of this place.
Approach, kind god: bestow your gifts on two,
    Your votaries, of different race
Made one, by love, by marriage, and by you.

# MARRIAGE AS A PROBLEM OF UNIVERSALS
*for Meera and Navin Govil*

    Marriage is where
The large abstractions we profess
Are put gently in their small place—
    The holist's stare
In love with Man has managed less
Than eyes that love one ageing face.

Marriage believes
The universals we desire
Are children of a worldly care —
    While Plato grieves
For stasis, the refining fire
Men pass through is the lives they share.

    Marriages move
Between the symbol and life's facts,
From Beauty to this troubled face —
    Though what we love
Is Truth, Truth flares and fades in acts
Of local, unrecorded grace.

# GOVERNMENT IN EXILE

Silence, and on the wall the photographs —
Farms, mountains, faces; the sad specifics
Corrode the heart, sharpen the will. Despair
Is shrugged away and stares one in the face.

Loyalty is poured out — a libation
To childhood villages, to stones, to trees.

# ST CHRISTOPHER

Curled fingers tighten in his curly hair:
But if, by any prescience, he knows
The nature of that burden He must bear
Whom now he bears, no recognition shows.

The weathered body and tenacious mind
Venture like partners with but one intent —
Lo, they are one, as cautiously they find
The safe stones through the unsafe element.

And thus, subsumed by what he does, made sure
That though his task is humble it is good,
He navigates toward the further shore —
Secure in skill and patient hardihood.

# REMBRANDT'S *RETURN OF THE PRODIGAL SON*

Age instinct with wisdom, love, bends towards
The sensual man, the penitent, and clasps
Him lightly by the shoulder-blades. In rags
The latter kneels and rests his close-cropped head
Against the Father's chest. Some watch, and one,
Whose face is lit, old as the Father, looks
With unobserved compassion at the scene.

His comprehension is the artist's own:
His silence and the Father's flood the frame
But cannot quite subdue the young man's sobs,
The fixed, sad past; the waste that love would heal.

# BAUCIS AND PHILEMON

Life lies to hand in hoe, spade, pruning-knife,
Plain wooden furniture and wattle walls,
In those unspoken words 'my husband' 'wife',
In one another's flesh which still recalls.

Beneath the map of age their savoured youth.
It is an ambience in which they move
Having no need to grasp or grub for truth,
It is the still persistence of their love.

That one should die before the other's death
And drain the world of meaning is their fear:
Their hope, to draw together their last breath
And leave the sunlight on a common bier.

Life is the meaning and the bread they share;
Because they need no Gods, the Gods are there.

# SEMELE

I imagine an English Semele —
A gawky girl who strayed beyond the town
Picking at stalks, alarmed by puberty . . .
Who by the handsome stranger's side lay down

And when he'd gone lay still in meadow-sweet
Knowing herself betrayed into the world —
Soft flesh suffused with summer's languid heat,
The clement light in which the ferns uncurled.

Both faded: meeting him again she sought
For that half-apprehended, longed-for power —
The glitter haunting her distracted thought
That seemed to peer from every leaf and flower,

The glory of the God . . . the girl became
The landscape's ghost, the sunlight's edgy flame.

# RICHARD DAVIS

'. . . minding to have sent to Qazvin Alexander Kitchin, whom God
took to His mercy the 23rd. October last: and before him departed
Richard Davis one of your mariners'.
Hakluyt, *Principal Voyages of the English Nation*

Our mariner's last landfall was this shore:
My namesake stood, four hundred years ago,
The empty Caspian at his back, and saw
A shelving view I intimately know —

Clean, silent air and noble poplar trees,
A marshy plain beyond which mountains rise,
The snow-line and the sky — all this he sees —
The colours fresh and calm before his eyes.

Fresh as your fading figure in my mind:
You look back to your little ship, then stare
As if the riches you had hoped to find
Were somehow present in the limpid air.

You walk towards the limits of my sight —
I see you stumble in the dusty light.

# CLIVE WILMER

## LIKENESS

In John the Pisan's statue at Siena
Of the wolf suckling Romulus and Remus,
In the anxious eyes and searching nose — the low
Thrust of her gaunt head from the prominent spine,

I see my own dog: she, though sweetly pampered,
Looked drained and scrawny when, still half a puppy,
With bleeding teats, she bowed beneath her instinct
To mother her first brood: I see this much

As he, the sculptor, must have seen the she-wolf
And every burden dour fate lays on us
In the bent head of a spurned mongrel bitch
Upon the streets of Pisa or Siena.


## TO THE UNDECEIVED

'. . . to play the game of energetic barbarism . . .
is, after all, a mental and moral impossibility.'
                              Borges, *Other Inquisitions*

You who invoke survival, and condemn
To ruin all the crumbling palaces
And shady temples, where I seek the dim
Outline of order; who trust, that there is

Sufficient order in the wilderness
To harbour man, that unhistoric air
May yield desolate words, that consciousness
Must be most lucid sunk in black despair;

You are the more deceived of us: the night
Of your dark souls inherits a desire
That burns in you, as it were for the sight
To wearied Romans of their world on fire.
What answer you are the oncoming hordes
You'd join, at length to fall on your own swords.

# THE DISENCHANTED

*On a painting by Atkinson Grimshaw,*
*'Liverpool Quay by Moonlight', 1887*

Riding at anchor ships from the New World,
Cargo-less now, sway, as in a trance;
Their lights float on a mist, their sails are furled;
They have disembarked both energy and distance.

Fated by deep unrest to haunt the quay
Aimless pilgrims, lit by the blear gaslight,
Emerge from haze, withdrawn in reverie:
      Exiles from day and night.

And at shop-windows they become transparent
To golden light that charms the brazen riches
There on display, before which they lament —
      As at vain reliquaries

That hold dead sanctity. They stare at distance
Imported by a manufactured world
To allure their wasting energy and substance
      By turning all to gold.

Bewitched but disenchanted lords they are,
Of a legendary treasure long since dispossessed,
Who drift with the dissolving atmosphere —
      Dim shades of the lost.

Only the lamp on a black, advancing coach
— Unearthly green! — can focus in reflection,
Composing all you see as you approach:
Light of the mind it stays from desolation.


# BIRD-WATCHER

It returns to the same nest. The watcher lies
Beneath spring brushwood to await its coming —
At watch so long he dreams himself becoming
Less than himself and more, the landscape's eyes.

Though far beyond his eyes, beyond the range
Of field-glasses, he knows it breaks no bonds:
Its instinct to his knowledge corresponds,
Riding the current of the season's change.

What is there in a small bird's blood that learns
To plot its course by sun and stars, being drawn
Yearly toward a lost, remembered dawn?
The watcher broods on this. The bird returns.

And all its colours flash where he attends —
A deep blue, mantling rust and white —, it sings
Caged in his retina; then, on curving wings,
Veers off to vanish where the human ends.

# IL PALAZZO DELLA RAGIONE

Passing the central Palace (called 'of Reason')
In Padua, daily I'd contemplate,
High on one wall among begrimed inscriptions,

Leaning as from a window, a gentleman
In Quattrocento costume — with a turban.
He smiles across distance, his hand raised in greeting.

Smiling as if at me, to bid me welcome
To a city, enlightened and humane,
Whose style I can neither touch nor imitate.

And though I would not say,
'This is a final wisdom,
As of Christ or the Buddha, on the Palace of Reason,'

Yet it seems he has a graciousness
Beyond our time to emulate,
Though one may celebrate.

That smile across the ages is intent
On courtesy. And nonetheless,
I suffer it as though it were contempt.

# HOMECOMING
*A Theme and Variations*

1 *Mid-winter*

The year goes out in wrath. And through the winter
Are scattered little days like cottages.
And lampless, hourless nights; and grey mornings,
Their indistinguishable images.

Summertime, autumn — time and season passing,
And brown death has seized on every fruit.
And new cold stars appear now in the darkness,
Unseen before, even from the ship's roof.

Pathless is every life. And every path
Bewildered. The end unknown. And whoso seeks
And finds a path finds that his utterance breaks
Off in sight of it, empty the hands he shakes.

2 *A Winter Evening*

When snow falls on pane and sill,
Long peals are borne on evening air;
The board is laid for many there
In a house provided well.

On their wanderings, several others
Come to the gate by dark ways.
Gold blossoms the tree of grace
Where cool sap in the earth gathers.

The wanderer quietly steps across
A threshold pain has turned to stone.
On the board glow bread and wine
In all the radiance of loss.

3 *A Threshold*

You, centaury, o lesser star,
You birch, you fern, you oak:
Near me you stay as I go far . . .
Home, into your snare we walk.

Black on a bearded palm tree
Hangs cherry-laurel bunched like grapes.
*I love, I hope, I believe . . .*
The small date, split open, gapes.

A saying speaks — to whom? To itself: *Servir*
*Dieu est régner . . .* I can
Read it, I can — it is coming clear —
Get out of Me-no-unnerstan.

*after Georg Heym, 'Mitte des Winters'*
*Georg Trakl, 'Ein Winterabend'*
*Paul Celan, 'Kermorvan'*

# THE PARABLE OF THE SOWER
*Stained glass in the Arts & Crafts style, set in a medieval church*

I

The sower goes out to sow. His sense and form
Move only in a landscape of stained glass;
  The leads like ivy stems,
  Enmeshing, bind him in.
Outside, it is afternoon; inside, the sun
Irradiates a face in shadow — eyes
  Inclined toward the earth
  Crimsoning underfoot.
The glory round about and through his limbs
Is vision in excess of daily need,
  Devotion in the work
  Dispersed beyond the seed.

II

Victorian glass of eighteen ninety-seven,
Replacing the clear light in the west wall
  In homage to a time
  That built as if for ever.
The vision is of a vision that transfigured
Perspectives on the bare field; but with skill
  The craftsman has contained,
  Edged, the unearthly glow.

His observation accurate, the self
A blemish that his labour should efface,
    Devotion to his craft
    Speaks through the pictured face.


III

The sower does not see the field he sows.
He walks in rapture, but his eyes are vague
    With sorrow not his own,
    That has no root in earth.
It is the craftsman's sorrow, for he gave
These paradisal colours to the earth
    But when he looked on earth
    He found an absence there.
Here wayside, thorn, good ground and stony ground
Are stained through with devotion, with his need
    For things to mean — the word
    Secreted in the seed.


# THE ADVENT CAROLS
*Aspiciens a longe*

I look from afar. We stand in darkness.
A people in exile, shall we hear good news,
Who, toward midnight, in mid-winter, sing?

Sing words to call a light out of the darkness
To thaw dulled earth, to unfold her fairest bud;
Our song holds faith that the Word will be made flesh.

Now we bear candles eastward, bear them into
Inviolate dark the Word should occupy:
Light disembodied swells the sanctuary

Where an old dream is mimed, without conviction,
Over again. I look from afar. Our sung words
Are herald angels, and they announce his name,

But lay no fleshly mantle on the King,
The one Word. And yet, in the song's rising
Is rapture, and dayspring in the mind's dark:

For the one sanctuary, now, is the word not
Made flesh — though it is big with child, invaded
By the dumb world that was before it was.


# ANTIPHONAL SONNETS
*Of John Taverner*


1

Suppose a man were dying and this sound
Washed over him: it would be like, not sleep,
Not dream, but setting eyes for the first time
On the world, ours, yet other. For the sense
Of things would be the things themselves and words
Would gem the melismatic harmony
Rarely, articulating it. The mind —
In a language, the great mass of whose words
Are shattered into vagrant syllables
By gay polyphony — would edge towards
The scope of revelation, which is speechless.
Now, in the place of death, an angel sits
And speaks to three who mourn of interim,
Announces that the second day is done.


2

This was the world: the word.
                              Gratuitous day,
Stained by a red or a blue glaze, confined
By aspiring stone to space with no horizon:
Earthly things that composed an allegory
Which guessed at heaven. He cast given speech
Against the bossed and starry vaults, shattered it
To falling fragments, harmonies — a fertile
Resonance, as much like beauty as like that
It seemed at length to mask: in empty space
A simple disembodied word, the truth.
Then beauty was the hoofbeats in the nave,
The radiant shower of glass, a mace that knocked
Devotion from her pedestal, the flames
That burnt the rood in the broad light of day.

# ROBERT WELLS

## FURTHER ON DOWN

The vine leaves cup their copper sulphate spray.
The mute plums loosen here. A swallowtail
Crawls by a hornet and a flat
Beetle varnished like a green toenail.
But hill should come over hill, bay over bay,
And the mist hide what we be the first to chart —

Here the only goodness is the sweat
Falling forward as the body leans to the pick.
Closer than a snake in its slippery skin
Senses the earth I want the feel of earth,
And hour after hour as if to exhaust the rock
The shaft jars at the blows I lie beneath.

The pick starts with sparks. I lift it, want to go
Further on down as if each blow
Suddenly might find out for me the ease
Of the mind's movement, and release
This force so that it lets the body go —
Further on down, as if to exhaust the rock.

## THE KNOT

The knot cuts across however far
You cut back the wood,
A deep engraining. The figure moving there
Is not where your passion centres
But is a likeness of the shape
That itself moves inside you.

Do not hope to get away.
It is with you like the beat of your blood
And in your nearest moment before you sleep
The sigh in the ear
Against the pillow, though you turn
And turn away from the sound.

# HIS THIRST

It was the utmost of his thirst
To set his mouth against the stream,
Leaning his hands on the wet rocks.
It was his nearest to content
To feel the inward cold slip down
And quiet his body with its touch.

# THE COLONIST

He seeks a manner cleanly lean and spare,
Self-disenchanted, separate as the air,
Bodily silence poised amid his blood,
A virtue that no memory shall elude.
And peace is strengthless. How shall it abide?
Like rhododendron on a waste hillside,
Hydras of foliage burnished in the wind,
Memory persists, is rooted in his mind:
A soil made up of tiny filaments
Fed on itself, grown matted tough and dense
That throws a blanket over beds of stone,
Tree-stumps, and where the fallen trunks lie prone;
And broad leaves still from every vigorous stem
Unfolding in the spell of their own dream,
Glossy ungovernable and wildly kempt.
What's virtue but a mask for self-contempt?
    Still sealed in fantasy by praise and smiles
The child devises shabby rituals
Whereby seducer and seduced are made
Partners in shame, each one the other's shade.

# THE HERO

I clothe your body nearer than the dust,
Liven your weariness and taste your thirst.
I am the touch of air, a breath indrawn.
Number the attributes but I have gone.

# BREAKFAST

The pasture is a faded white.
Even the food palls
At the mountain's height by the spring,
A loaf in halves, unwrapped
From a blue cloth.
                    Oil and salt,
Raw ham. Sitting apart
To let the horse drink unscared
They brood what dream was broken
When mother or wife
Called them at four.


# THE ATTRIBUTES

1

Here are the path, the field. He takes this way
Setting his footprints in the spidery dew
Hunched from the rain, a sack about his shoulders
Lost as he moves, the sun's automaton.

Only the attributes can be expressed,
The body's useless grace, its constancy
Where impulse has no strength and these enough
To bear the sense of his surrendered soul.


2

His clothing mutes his skin as fate his soul
Gathering sweat and dust. Body and land
Touch on its reticence and are withheld,
Join there in secrecy and are absorbed,

So that he stays both weathered and unformed
And like these stones that go to make the walls,
Grizzled and worn but if you turn them over
Still white and even, still of the riverbed.

3

He watches daylight empty from the fields
That run to waste beyond the worked confines.
Their strengthless fancy was his thoughts' reserve
Softening each gesture with a fallow grace.

His disaffection is the wind that thickens
Amid the hazel scrub on his path home
Unfed, unwashed, the latest passer there
Whispering that body is the commonest thing.

4

Weakness commands. His strength is servitude,
Limbs that are matched against the endless clay,
Reproach that loiters where the brown back strains
And nothing sweetens, nothing is brought to him.

Diving into the cold, his startled blood
Shrinks and dilates again and rediscovers
A sobered joy, or crouching toward the stream
He starts to wash and then forgets to move.

## THE AXEHANDLE

Calling my eyes back from the sea
—With adoration I watched the horizon lift
Above the headland, far up against the sky —
And looking instead for a human token
Even at this distance, to hold me back,

I noticed the axe where I had put it aside
— How the balanced ashwood handle
Was like a limb with its muscle shaped to use,
An arm graceful and certain with hillside labour
Evidencing the generations of hands.

# AFTER HAYMAKING

The last bale placed, he stretched out in the hay.
    Its warmth and his were one.
He watched the fields beneath the weakening day
And felt his skin still burning with the sun.

When it was dusk, he moved. Between his skin
    And clothes the sweat ran cold.
He trembled as he felt the air begin
To touch and touch for what it could not hold.


# VENDEMMIA

And your dialect blurred with locality, I think,
As the grapes with mist. We work along the rows
Stripping the bunches from the vines, while I puzzle
For sense in this tender meaningless conceit.


# SHAPE OF AIR

It has lighted on you, this shape of air.
I don't want you to know that it is there:
Not yours or mine, as by the gate you stand
That divides the mountain from the worked land
And the first light of day, neither shade nor shine,
Shows through your open shirt your body's line.
The stones, the coppice, the inconsequent trees,
The cold fountain by the path, where blackberries
Rot on the bushes unpicked, and before noon
The cattlemen, work finished, will rest from the sun:
How casually you come here, bring that shape,
Stretch in the grass, drink from the metal cup
Its cramping mouthful; certainly of this place,
Your muscle-rumoured limbs and quiet face
And ready glee. O beat the earth at a joke
With open palm, it was the same smile broke
An age ago here, and the same shape lit.
The same hope as mine was effaced by it.

# GRAN SASSO

Around the highest village, fields are ploughed
However pale the soil and frequent the stones.

Old habits huddle between old walls. The church bell,
Slight and unresonant, is a familiar sound.

Above the village, the final mountains lift.
Who climbs them feels his life thin out like air

And finds beyond the ridge a treeless meadow
Without a trace of history or occupation.

Then the summit, gross blunted rock that has shed
The last vestige of anything but itself.


# FOR PASOLINI

Vecchio ragazzo di Casarsa, dear protagonist,
Where shall we find the like of your intelligence?
The hunters who come here on Sunday with their dogs and guns
Are not enough to keep the forest paths open.
Two years untrodden, and bramble will cover the track,
The broom lean across. They were paved once with stones
Packed in together to make rough and narrow highways,
Loosened now, a rubble, a watercourse, except
For some short stretches where the old work has held.
If someone climbs up between the crests of the ridge,
Pushing through bracken that drenches his boots and clothes,
He will guess perhaps that this was the charcoal-burners' place:
But who can imagine now what their lives were, find more
Than that if he scratches the surface of the mounded green
He turns up blacker earth — their trace? O early bodies
Moving amid the dark as it thins. O quiet voices.
When ignorant beauty chances to conjure back to life
The shape present in the air, who will be here to know it?

# DERELICT LANDSCAPE

The rock that has broken and toppled across the track
Where cattlemen drove their herds will never be moved.

The manners of the old men coming in from the fields
At nightfall are sweeter than the bodies of the young.


# AT LICENZA

1

The floor of the path in autumn:
Crisping walnut leaves, cast chestnut husks,
The chicory flower blue on its stem,
White stones —
                    A sheen on surfaces
Like a happiness
That cannot find its cause.

At the moment of striking the light draws away.
The things are shown and yet not reached.


2

Dusk: they bring the animals in.
The horses, for all their strength and size,
Are led by a small boy.

Turning into the road from the steep track
He stops at the parapet of the bridge,
Climbs on the back of one and sits astride.

The bridle rope coiled at his wrist,
He nudges the great flanks with his heels.

# MEDIAN PALACE

*in Luristan*

A king over shepherds: here he built his house,
His columned hall, roof set with painted tiles,
    The master of an acreage
As far as he could see from the towered walls.

By what trust or ignorance did he build and live?
We drink at the spring that fed his walled garden;
    We watch the scarlet hoopoe
Strutting in the court where once it drew his eyes.

How firm they must have stood, the bulwarked rooms,
Refuge from sun and snow and the great sky,
    Before the frail balance
Of circumstance was jarred, and shook them down;

A layer of ash which we brush gently clear,
A hillock, pale earth melting to pale earth.
    Did he foresee the fall,
The strangers who would explain themselves by swords?

I turn the tiles up where the roof crashed in
And find an earthenware fetish, a foot,
    Its sandal bound by snakes,
And a bronze pin capped by a staring head.

# JOHN ASH

## EARLY VIEWS OF MANCHESTER AND PARIS: FIRST VIEW

It makes us uncomfortable: the pillars
and shadowed arches of these monuments
to commerce are a furniture we can't
or daren't throw out. Hard not to admire
such a total dedication to redundancy, —

as if the whole city were a railway station
and the line diverted. In the photographs
of that age the only people to be visible
were those who stood for long periods
without moving. Only when it began
to die did the running mob appear
as dim smudges on a bridge in Paris.

And now are they visible?
Do they move freely?

## *from* 'THE RAIN'

We have to love the past
it is our invention. Perhaps, after all
forgiveness is the proper attitude
and we should not abolish history but make a space in it
that will contain both the philosophies
of eighteenth-century boudoirs and the Kingdom of Meroe,
the Empire of Songhoi . . . and the place
where the last Carib leapt to his death
and the place where the last prince of the Palaeologi
is buried are the same in our understanding:
the sky is the same and the sea. So
the primitive thumb-piano hacked from the edge
of your mother's kitchen table can now encompass
all the masterpieces of our literature, —
the great fugues, consumptive nocturnes and love elegies . . .
It is right that we don't know what to expect, —
this revival of polyphony could alter entirely

the simple relation of sound to colour, or sharpen
to the fineness of a stylus our dulled anticipation
of the storm that still holds off, —
flickering and crashing in some closed department of time
like a shoe shifting in its box, already entered
by the idea of the foot. We don't forget
that the light comes from inside, is an oblong of limited extent
with thickets bristling at its edges, but are still moved
by the idea of creatures and places that do not exist
and are necessary: we don't believe in them
but this rain is weeping nonetheless and the flowers grief, —
the wilted petals are the colour of hospital corridors, but the scent, —
the scent of the flowers is like a murmurous greeting
in a language you do not understand, in the bald dictionary sense of
    understanding,
but its mere sound creates fresh sentiments, lithe figures
for the alcoves prepared long in advance, capped by the shell of
    desire.


# THE NORTHERN SYMPHONIES

The pines shiver expecting winter
vanishing in mist

moths circle the lights of railway platforms
at intervals through a thousand, two thousand miles

The peasants are painting dolls —
dolls within dolls

the children of aristocrats
are collecting mushrooms and butterflies

the river erases all the names
of adolescents written out in the sand

and their letters remain undiscovered
as the wooden bridges split slowly apart

The empty palace is painted green and gold
snow has fallen in the square

a crowd brings down the statue at its centre
soon no-one can remember

whether it represented
a man or a woman

O how cold the air is!
what bitter tiredness

and how unexpectedly sad
the faces of the crowd . . .

There is a loud cracking sound
as if a great river suddenly thawed
as if a ship fired all its guns at once

an enormous mirror stands up
and in an instant dissolves
running in all directions like spilt mercury

melting snow washes blood from the birch copse —
how will the new life begin?


# THEM/THERE
*to the memory of Erik Satie*

What are the people like there? How do they live? . . . I'll admit I've
never been there, but that won't stop me telling you all about it.

The people there weep often, alone in rooms with candles and old
books. In their terrible Augusts they make black entries in their
diaries. Their songs are doleful but the dances at funerals can be very
lively, — danced to the rhythm of whips, gourds and snares — and
the colour of mourning is ochre. . . . They are fervently religious
yet their government is atheist: to discourage worship the roofs have
been removed from all their churches. But any government is
provisional. Each summer, and sometimes during bad winters there
are riots in the streets of their windswept and lacustrine capital.
There are so many informers, however, that the police always know
in advance the exact time and place. Thus everything is done
properly: vendors may set up their stalls, street musicians choose
their stands, and respectable families gather in perfect safety to watch

the instructive spectacle. . . . Tobacco and sheep are the basis of the economy. Out of patriotic duty everyone there chain smokes at incredible speed: they regard the medical reports with furious disdain, and their ceilings are stained a deep, yellowish-brown (like papyrus scrolls from the cemeteries of Fayyum). Their sheep are, without question, the shaggiest and most unkempt in the world, — each animal a mobile continent colonised by vast tribes of ticks. . . . They are always washing things in water so soapy it is barely fluid, and yet nothing ever seems clean. And they think of themselves as Hellenes! Arbiters! . . . In their typical symphonic music a huge, squelching adagio like a sea-slug is followed by epileptic dances, catastrophic marches, — the whole concluding in a welter of chromatic swoons. Their orchestras are very large. They play everything *fortissimo*. (And — horrors! — they re-orchestrate Mozart!) Their national anthem is an arrangement of the mastodon-trumpet theme from Scriabin's 'Poem of Ecstasy'. (When the massed bands of the Republic begin to play this it is difficult to persuade them to stop. . . .) And yet, strange to relate, they possess singing voices of an exceptional and haunting beauty. . . . Their buildings are either hen-coops or Piranesi dungeons, Nissen huts or Sammarran mausoleums. . . . Their poets write constantly of their failed marriages, failing health, unhappy childhoods and — for variety — the apostrophes to stars of laundresses and cabmen. . . . It rains often, yet the vegetation is sparse in many areas and the summers can be oppressively hot. Steam rises in great clouds from their low roofs, and from the many balconies where drenched furs are hung to dry. Steam rises and moisture drips ceaselessly onto their unsurfaced streets in which a score of jeeps and hay-carts have their wheels stuck fast. Their flags hang always at half mast. As if ashamed their rivers vanish underground. . . . In the south of the country there are extensive lakes of warm, grey mud. . . . The train there moves in fantastic, slow loops, — a baroque embroidery expressing an infinite reluctance to arrive. They think, with good reason, that the world is forgetting them. . . . They greet each dawn with a chorus of deafening expectorations.


# A BEAUTY

It was an intellectual face, —
white, with the mute look of a rose about to be doused
with a powerful insecticide,
and she never understood why, in her presence

*perfectly sensible men* would lose all control. What
was it she *did?* It cannot
have been anything she said. . . .

Further incidents: she borrowed the old earl's Rolls
to take her to the station, and stole
his breakfast kipper to eat on the train;
the whole family had a wonderful time that summer
in the Tuscan palace lent by an infatuated count
except that all the floors were so highly polished
that, by the end of their stay, sprained wrists and broken ankles
were scattered through their ranks like floral tributes
at the end of a charity matinée;
she was horrified when her younger brother's hair
was cut sort, declaring it 'an atrocity', —
and never forgot this. . . .

Everything worried her, even the great rose–windows of the
    cathedral, —
but there was always the consolation of 'the dear countryside',
rolling away like vellum or old velvet into a distance where,
unquestionably, something very nasty and probably foreign was
continually going on, — a kind of dust storm, an old argument
the wind wouldn't let drop, which she wasn't about to lend an ear to.

In 1917 Regie wrote to her: 'You remember Roughton?
Joined the Balloon Corps. Poor chap. Shot down
last week at 6,000 feet. He landed not far from me, —
shockingly foreshortened, but still recognisable by his cigarette
    case.'

The man she eventually married was a hopeless drunk.
She hardly seemed to notice. Despite this,
and his rumoured womanising, the marriage 'worked'.
During her second war she kept goats — 'such
*useful* animals' — and wrote to the ministry advising
the placing of giant magnets in the parks of the capital
to attract the German bombs there, —
'thus sparing many lives and many fine old buildings'.

Like her beauty, her myopia was legendary:
often she would sail past acquaintances of several years —
quite unawares, leaving a fine foam of grievances glittering in her
    wake.

In her extreme old age she still posed for photographs
wearing a large hat trimmed with brilliant blue ostrich feathers
(this is a form of courage ought not to be disdained), —
her autobiography (ghost-written)
might have been called 'A Milliner's Chronicle', or
'The Philosophy of Hats', — recording, as it did,
the different phases of the horrible century she lived in
in terms of face-veils, lace-work, birds' wings, pins, and fake
  collapsing flowers:
a method not without advantages. As good as any, you might
  say. . . .


# POOR BOY: PORTRAIT OF A PAINTING

Difficult to say what all of this is all about.
Being young. Or simply arrogance, lack of patience —

a misunderstanding about what the word maturity
can mean when exchanged among 'real' adults. . . .

I don't know what kind of plant that is, but it
is green and has a small red flower

and the glass it strives towards is latticed,
yellowish and cracked. Beyond it

roofs are bunched together like boats
in a popular harbour
and through it the inevitable light falls. . . .

And the light is art! It is arranged *so,*
over the bed and the pale dead boy,
his astonishing red hair, the shirt rumpled like sculpture,

the breeches. . . . The breeches are a problem:
no one can decide whether they are blue
or mauve. Versions differ. But the light

is faultless. It can hit anything
whatever the distance, —
for example, the squashed triangle of white lining

to the stiff, mulberry coloured dressing–gown,
the torn–up sheets of poems or pornography,
the oriental blade of pallor above
the boy's large, left eye-lid or even the small, brown
dope bottle lying on the scrubbed floor
almost at the bottom of the picture. Of course

much depends on the angle. Much remains
obscure, but this only enhances
these significant islands of brilliance,
exposed and absolutely
vulnerable to our interpretation:

there is nowhere he can hide the hand that rests
just above his stomach as if he still felt horribly ill.


# AN IDYLL FOR ELLIE AND RUTH

The bed had a person in it.
The sun was climbing through warm mist.

It had been raining, now it was snowing.
The book on the table was wrapped in a bright flag of convenience.
Two small girls, dressed in blue and red nightgowns
were arranging the cards in the shape of a fat man
who seemed to be signalling desperately, —

'Over here! Over here! . . . You know me,
you surely must remember; we met on Thursday, —
O, it was a day of unforced amity! the sky
was veined like a slice of marble or blue cheese;
you told me to give up my job in the bank and spend more
    time in the greenhouse, —
also, I was to eat less and read more. . . .'

Twigs snapped in the fire. The fault opened like a sigh
and the whole suburb swayed gently south,
dislodging from the breasts of several matrons, pearls
that rolled under the wheels of speeding cars. Suddenly

everything was tired and wanted to go to bed.
We did, and you. Also they. And it.

Curtains began to blow. Birds were standing
very watchful and still, in the heaped snow. The scene
shuddered like shoulders
when the sneeze can no longer be suppressed:

general embarrassment — a rosey blush —
consumed the features of the day,

which is to say, it was now evening
where it had been morning.


# THE STRANGER IN THE CORRIDOR
*'O sole, true Something — This!. . . .'* S. T. Coleridge

With vague attributes, they all wander in here
at one time or another. Often
I wish they would stay longer, if not to speak,
then perhaps to take on some more certain form, —

a swirl of colour (orange or green) in an otherwise
transparent marble that has just emerged,
of its own volition, from years of exile under the sofa.
And why has it come to us at this moment?

The unimpressive apparition might mean something, —
for an unexpected pause in the recitation of a letter
can have more power to disturb than a whole succession
of subsiding Valhallas, and we can barely read the words

announcing the discovery of the lost girl,
the mystery of the mésalliance. Is it the dim light?
Or tears of the sort that are compared to pearls? . . .

We care about this more than a little
but will never know: this evening's visitor comes as an odour
of freshly baked bread that follows me
down the narrow corridor from the little bedroom lined with books,
and there is nowhere it can come from! It seems
friendly enough, 'concerned' even. A response from the air.

Or something that has stepped outside of me for a moment
to 'take the air' like a fluttering heroine after the execution
of some especially fevered nocturne, in search of refreshment
to stretch its limbs a little, and to remind me that I have been

Neglecting it. And I *have* been neglecting it. This is obvious,
for it most resembles a guest at a crowded party whom you have
    introduced to no one:
a charming guest but with a look of reproach.

I have forgotten so many things and this is one
and wants to take its place among the salvaged, —
among flowers from the fifties or the colours of a paintbox,
under the brim of a hat, beside a gold river at the heart of an old
    province
that is growing with each intake of breath
as the fresh odour spreads, claiming the most impervious objects,
reviving the colours that had begun
to fade to white scarves of the death of this place
that is now big as a democracy, vivid as a nettle's sting, —
and we cry out, hurt! The task ahead
is momentous but pleasurable: you have to invent, or —
which may be the same thing — remember
the language of this place, its peculiar history, cuisine and carnivals;
what people did in its eighteenth century; whether it is
appropriate to talk of 'serfdom' after the close of its nineteenth
    century,
the ambiguous relationship of this to the rise of a bourgeoisie. . . .
And so on. You might also prepare new
and superbly accurate editions of dissonant masterpieces
by its early church composers, or discover
in a foxhole, the last act, lost for decades, of its most famous opera.
When you have done all this, conducted a census
and completed the catalogue of native birds, you will be able
to find the place where, in the midst of this much folded and
pleated landscape   the loaf rises like a monument:

now free from hunger and confinement,
we inhabit its shadow.


# THE GOODBYES

1   Again, the weather's wrecked the picnic.
    All those drenched frocks,
      tomato slices in flooded bowls —

so English! the clouds, the downpour
as evasive terms
for a continuing epic of bad faith
and commonplace ill-feeling. . . .

2   Yes, something *has* changed
    irreversibly. It speaks out of silence
    like a radio announcer
    off-cue. Time to remove the varnish? Yes. . . .

3   All departures cancelled:
    the pillars in the painting are grey
    and the sails of fishing boats
    drawn in with no hope of unfurling, —
    blue cranes of the container–depot
    motionless. Only the immense
    sandstone cathedral looks as if it might move —
    gliding off, a gothic liner, leaving
    the city burning behind it. . . .

4   Dun cows like stalled cars
    are dumped in all the streams:
    someone has *smoked* the landscape.

5   The glass graph-paper of office buildings catches
    no sun this evening, and this expresses
    everything we feel about the situation and do not understand,
    'How could you love a person like him or like her?
    They are ignorant, – they think *all* Italians are Catholic.
    Their blond hair gets into everything, even sleep. . . .'

6   With things as they are it's difficult not
    to feel like a newly arrived exile
    even though you've lived here for years.
    Principal cities are renamed and history
    slides into a dull dream of foreknowledge
    in which past mistakes are cancelled.
    Who are these heroes appearing in the false guise
    of youth? these avatars of
    expediency? No one is convinced. Even
    the sky is discoloured
    like the pages of a novel left open at a window, —
    the plot so mechanical every word or sigh
    fell with a thud to rot slowly where it fell,

staining the carpet at the place
where the corpse is marked in chalk.

7   And the clouds! The clouds!
O, a thousand sobbing goodbyes!

Overweight and weeping bitterly
they are dragged off to interrogation:

they confess everything,
including your address. . . .

8   A fog is expected, —
the first 'real pea-souper' in years.
'You can't rely on the weather. . . .'
Everyone agrees on this
while the window darkens
like someone's mother's brow in splendid
anger: 'Child! O
ingrate! My lichen! Little cuckoo, go
into the world: it is
a narrow corridor and we do not know its end, —

unless it be this blurred picture
of a river or a tree, branching in Africa. . . .'

9   Voices rise in confusion, —
counterpoint of amateurs. Talk
turns to the furniture of permanence.
Contracts are signed, houses change hands
(hands change houses) but yours
is not (is never) the face seen at the window
advertising with a cold smile
its new contentment. That smile! You'd think
death were abolished, and people
not starving with infinite slowness —
là-bas, là-bas: their hands make a thorn-bush
on which your morning paper is impaled.

10   Friend, you'd better board up that window,
*never know what might go down to-night* —

an ice factory is planned for your garden
a steel mill for your living room

a six-lane highway for the hall
and even now, directly beneath your feet
huge coal-seams are being explored. . . .

The walls are shaking. The light
is drunk. Goodbye.

11   This is only goodbye —

a handkerchief like a white wing
a tear in a bottle, a moist hand
encountered in a hotel foyer,

the goodbye of silence,
late music and exhausted nerves

goodbye stretched to the furthest point
of perspective, where
the small spaces of our lives
submit to immensity —

the grass that continues as an unbroken blue undulation
over mountain ranges and stepped cities of moss

the goodbye of calls
crossed and misdirected
like the preparatory sketch
for the beast in a fable, —

bearded with sharp ears
the face a kind of mesh that shines towards us
as the goodbye
of everything we are uncertain of

the goodbye that leaves you ruined
(split cast for a bronze figure of defeat)

the goodbye of goodbyes
it wants no more —

the goodbye of words
that rub themselves out

the goodbye like a blank stair-
case leading
back into whatever you were.

# FERNS AND THE NIGHT

*'Und wir hörten sie noch von ferne*
*Trotzig singen im Wald.'*

This is the sort of place you might arrive at after a long journey
involving the deaths of several famous monsters,
only to be disappointed almost to the point of grief.

Heavy clouds hang in a clump above a wide, perfectly level plain
which is the image of a blank mind. Night is falling.
There is a wooden house, a lighted porch: it is a scene of 'marvellous
    simplicity'. —
Too marvellous perhaps: the very grain of the wood offers itself
for our admiration, and the light has such 'warmth'
it is hard to restrain tears. The clouds are now distinctly purple,
agitated, — a kind of frantically stirred borsch, suitable backdrop
for some new opera's Prelude of Foreboding, but not for this
    ambiguous scene
of severity tempered by domestic tenderness, in which we find
the 'young mother' looking for her child. . . . He has run off
into deep woods nearby, leaving his blue train crashed on the lawn.
She calls his name, but after the third call it becomes difficult or
    exotic music,
a series in retrograde inversion, an entry in the catalogue of
    unknown birds:
she is already elsewhere, her torch illuminating the pure,
chlorophyll-green ferns of a forest, and the torch itself, a flame. . . .

She finds that her bare feet are wet and that she is looking into a
    puddle,
Seeing the clouds reflected and her face (the moon also). She calls
    again
but has forgotten where she is, or whose name she is calling. Her
    own perhaps?
The wooden house, the lighted porch seem unreachable, —
artfully lit, a glassed-in exhibit in some future museum of the
    human.
Ferns and the night conceal the child whose laughter distantly
    reaches her.

# JAMES FENTON

## A GERMAN REQUIEM

'For as at a great distance of place, that which wee look at, appears dimme,
and without distinction of the smaller parts; and as Voyces grow weak,
and inarticulate: so also after great distance of time, our imagination of the
Past is weak; and wee lose (for example) of Cities wee have seen, many
particular Streets; and of Actions, many particular Circumstances. This
decaying sense, when wee would express the thing it self, (I mean fancy
it selfe,) wee call Imagination, as I said before: But when we would
express the decay, and signifie that the Sense is fading, old, and past, it
is called Memory. So that Imagination & Memory, are but one
thing . . .'

Hobbes, Leviathan

It is not what they built. It is what they knocked down.
It is not the houses. It is the spaces between the houses.
It is not the streets that exist. It is the streets that no longer exist.
It is not your memories which haunt you.
It is not what you have written down.
It is what you have forgotten, what you must forget.
What you must go on forgetting all your life.
And with any luck oblivion should discover a ritual.
You will find out that you are not alone in the enterprise.
Yesterday the very furniture seemed to reproach you.
Today you take your place in the Widow's Shuttle.

★

The bus is waiting at the southern gate
To take you to the city of your ancestors
Which stands on the hill opposite, with gleaming pediments,
As vivid as this charming square, your home.
Are you shy? You should be. It is almost like a wedding,
The way you clasp your flowers and give a little tug at your veil. Oh,
The hideous bridesmaids, it is natural that you should resent them
Just a little, on this first day.
But that will pass, and the cemetery is not far.

Here comes the driver, flicking a toothpick into the gutter,
His tongue still searching between his teeth.
See, he has not noticed you. No one has noticed you.
It will pass, young lady, it will pass.


★

How comforting it is, once or twice a year,
To get together and forget the old times.
As on those special days, ladies and gentlemen,
When the boiled shirts gather at the graveside
And a leering waistcoat approaches the rostrum.
It is like a solemn pact between the survivors.
The mayor has signed it on behalf of the freemasonry.
The priest has sealed it on behalf of all the rest.
Nothing more need be said, and it is better that way –


★

The better for the widow, that she should not live in fear of surprise.
The better for the young man, that he should move at liberty
    between the armchairs,
The better that these bent figures who flutter among the graves
Tending the nightlights and replacing the chrysanthemums
Are not ghosts,
That they shall go home.
The bus is waiting, and on the upper terraces
The workmen are dismantling the houses of the dead.


★

But when so many had died, so many and at such speed,
There were no cities waiting for the victims.
They unscrewed the name-plates from the shattered doorways
And carried them away with the coffins.
So the squares and parks were filled with the eloquence of young
    cemeteries:
The smell of fresh earth, the improvised crosses
And all the impossible directions in brass and enamel.


★

'Doctor Gliedschirm, skin specialist, surgeries 14–16 hours or by
    appointment.'
Professor Sargnagel was buried with four degrees, two associate
    memberships
And instructions to tradesmen to use the back entrance.
Your uncle's grave informed you that he lived on the third floor, left.
You were asked please to ring, and he would come down in the lift
To which one needed a key . . .


★


Would come down, would ever come down
With a smile like thin gruel, and never too much to say.
How he shrank through the years.
How you towered over him in the narrow cage.
How he shrinks now . . .


★


But come. Grief must have its term? Guilt too, then.
And it seems there is no limit to the resourcefulness of recollection.
So that a man might say and think:
When the world was at its darkest,
When the black wings passed over the rooftops
(And who can divine His purposes?) even then
There was always, always a fire in this hearth.
You see this cupboard? A priest-hole!
And in that lumber-room whole generations have been housed and
    fed.
Oh, if I were to begin, if I were to begin to tell you
The half, the quarter, a mere smattering of what we went through!


★


His wife nods, and a secret smile,
Like a breeze with enough strength to carry one dry leaf
Over two pavingstones, passes from chair to chair.
Even the enquirer is charmed.
He forgets to pursue the point.
It is not what he wants to know.
It is what he wants not to know.
It is not what they say.
It is what they do not say.

# CAMBODIA

One man shall smile one day and say goodbye.
Two shall be left, two shall be left to die.

One man shall give his best advice.
Three men shall pay the price.

One man shall live, live to regret.
Four men shall meet the debt.

One man shall wake from terror to his bed.
Five men shall be dead.

One man to five. A million men to one.
And still they die. And still the war goes on.

# IN A NOTEBOOK

*There was a river overhung with trees*
*With wooden houses built along its shallows*
*From which the morning sun drew up a haze*
*And the gyrations of the early swallows*
*Paid no attention to the gentle breeze*
*Which spoke discreetly from the weeping willows.*
*There was a jetty by the forest clearing*
*Where a small boat was tugging at its mooring.*

*And night still lingered underneath the eaves.*
*In the dark houseboats families were stirring*
*And Chinese soup was cooked on charcoal stoves.*
*Then one by one there came into the clearing*
*Mothers and daughters bowed beneath their sheaves.*
*The silent children gathered round me staring*
*And the shy soldiers setting out for battle*
*Asked for a cigarette and laughed a little.*

*From low canoes old men laid out their nets*
*While on the bank young boys with lines were fishing.*
*The wicker traps were drawn up by their floats.*
*The girls stood waist-deep in the river washing*

*Or tossed the day's rice on enamel plates*
*And I sat drinking bitter coffee wishing*
*The tide would turn to bring me to my senses*
*After the pleasant war and the evasive answers.*

There was a river overhung with trees.
The girls stood waist-deep in the river washing,
And night still lingered underneath the eaves
While on the bank young boys with lines were fishing.
Mothers and daughters bowed beneath their sheaves
While I sat drinking bitter coffee wishing —
And the tide turned and brought me to my senses.
The pleasant war brought the unpleasant answers:

The villages are burnt, the cities void;
The morning light has left the river view;
The distant followers have been dismayed;
And I'm afraid, reading this passage now,
That everything I knew has been destroyed
By those whom I admired but never knew;
The laughing soldiers fought to their defeat
And I'm afraid most of my friends are dead.

# THE SKIP

I took my life and threw it on the skip,
Reckoning the next-door neighbours wouldn't mind
If my life hitched a lift to the council tip
With their dry rot and rubble. What you find

With skips is — the whole community joins in.
Old mattresses appear, doors kind of drift
Along with all that won't fit in the bin
And what the bin-men can't be fished to shift.

I threw away my life, and there it lay
And grew quite sodden. 'What a dreadful shame,'
Clucked some old bag and sucked her teeth: 'The way
The young these days . . . no values . . . me, I blame . . .'

But I blamed no one. Quality control
Had loused it up, and that was that. 'Nough said.
I couldn't stick at home. I took a stroll
And passed the skip, and left my life for dead.

Without my life, the beer was just as foul,
The landlord still as filthy as his wife,
The chicken in the basket was an owl,
And no one said: 'Ee, Jim-lad, whur's thee life?'

Well, I got back that night the worse for wear,
But still just capable of single vision;
Looked in the skip; my life — it wasn't there!
Some bugger'd nicked it — *without* my permission.

Okay, so I got angry and began
To shout, and woke the street. Okay. *Okay!*
*And* I was sick all down the neighbour's van.
*And* I disgraced myself on the par-*kay*.

And then . . . you know how if you've had a few
You'll wake at dawn, all healthy, like sea breezes,
Raring to go, and thinking: 'Clever you!
You've got away with it.' And then, oh Jesus,

It hits you. Well, that morning, just at six
I woke, got up and looked down at the skip.
There lay my life, still sodden, on the bricks;
There lay my poor old life, arse over tip.

Or was it mine? Still dressed, I went downstairs
And took a long cool look. The truth was dawning.
Someone had just exchanged my life for theirs.
Poor fool, I thought — I should have left a warning.

Some bastard saw my life and thought it nicer
Than what he had. Yet what he'd had seemed fine.
He'd never caught his fingers in the slicer
The way I'd managed in that life of mine.

His life lay glistening in the rain, neglected,
Yet still a decent, an authentic life.
Some people I can think of, I reflected
Would take that thing as soon as you'd say Knife.

It seemed a shame to miss a chance like that.
I brought the life in, dried it by the stove.
It looked so fetching, stretched out on the mat.
I tried it on. It fitted, like a glove.

And now, when some local bat drops off the twig
And new folk take the house, and pull up floors
And knock down walls and hire some kind of big
Container (say, a skip) for their old doors,

I'll watch it like a hawk, and every day
I'll make at least — oh — half a dozen trips.
I've furnished an existence in that way.
You'd not believe the things you find on skips.

# A TERMINAL MORAINE

It's simple but I find it hard to explain
Why I should wish to go from the moraine.

Below me in the wide plains I can see
Straight roads through flat fields, a measured sea.

At night with its orange lamps the city raised
To a dome, the fields lost under haze.

Above where a vein of granite and a stream
Are indistinguishable sometimes the crags seem

To totter against the moving clouds. Those dots
Of orange represent climbers on the rocks.

At night I can see nothing of the valley behind,
Though from the bleating of the sheep my mind

Constructs with points as on a graph the curved
Recess. A stream gathers and swerves

A few yards before my hill. Here there are trees,
Mainly pines, and every sudden breeze

Is amplified for my benefit. I listen and in the deep
Of the night, when I am alone, I landscape my sleep.

Daylight brings company or distraction: clouds
Passing, the lichen on the rock with its loud

Disturbing yellow. Shutting my eyes
I am never alone. Each element vies,

Whether it is a birch-leaf turning in the sun
Or a car on the road. There are boys with guns

And hikers in bright socks. I do not rise early.
I eat in an orderly fashion and think clearly.

I arrange objects in rooms according to a design
And am usually presentable. If the prospect is fine

For a walk, I naturally go. There will always be
The evening for work. My decisions are free.

Except when visitors cry off or friends leave
After long weekends it is enough to deceive

The mind into employment and to give shape to thought.
And if this I could have its way it ought

To turn as a wheel in a millstream. There is peace
In this valley. Why not enjoy it? while the trees

Enchant my sleep and I become a thing
Of caves and hollows, mouths where the winds sing.

But when a car is on the road I hear
My heart beat faster as it changes gear.


# THE KINGFISHER'S BOXING GLOVES

(le martin-pêcheur et ses gants bourrés)
*after Baudelaire*

The walrus stretches forth a wrinkled hand.
The petrel winks a dull, mascaraed eye.
Dusk comes softly, treading along the sand.
Along the wet spar and the hornbeam sky
Night is secreted in the orbit's gland.
The alligator yawns and heaves a sigh.
Between its teeth, black as an upright grand,
The mastik bird performs its dentistry.

So much sand that a man at night becomes
A perfect hourglass. Out among the dunes
They stretch the vellum on the savage drums.
The hotel bar is hushed. The bootboy croons
Softly. The manager completes his sums
And shuts the register. The end of June's
The end of his season. The song he hums
Clashes at midnight with the savage tunes.

It is the marram grass, the marram grass
That soughs beneath my balcony all night,
That claws the webbed feet of the beasts that pass,
That irritates the nostrils till they fight.
Fed up with sand, tired of treading on glass,
I take the coach and leave tomorrow night
For colder, milder northern climes, alas
With friends of whom I cannot bear the sight.

The diamond cutter working for de Beers,
The lady with the yashmak from Zem-Zem,
The tattooed man, the girl with jutting ears,
The lovely bishop with the kiss-worn gem,
That pair of cataleptic engineers,
I throw out pontoon bridges to meet them
And take on new, funicular veneers,
Thanking my stars that this is just pro tem.

The cicerone is unknown to flap,
The sort of chap who never makes a slip.
He can provide the only useful map.
He tells the men how much and when to tip.
He buys the sort of rope that will not snap
On the descent. He tells you where to grip.
That it's the thirteenth step that brings the trap.
That smugglers sweat along the upper lip.

For this, much thanks. The way is often steep
And rust betrays the pitons of the blind.
The pollen count is up. The folding jeep
Sticks in the mud and must be left behind.
An engineer is murdered in his sleep.
The bishop owns a gun, owns up, is fined.
The other engineer begins to weep
And finally admits he's changed his mind.

'So soon!' the bishop cries, 'Come off it, Keith.
It's several hours too early to be scared.
The breasts are all behind us and the see-th-
rough skirts long past, their trials and dangers dared.'
(Up flies the kingfisher. It bares its teeth,
With orange laughter lines and nostrils flared.
Its long crow's feet are spreading out beneath.)
'I would have stayed if I had thought you cared.

'I would have been the party's life and soul,
But all you wanted was a bed of nails.
I would have chopped the logs and fetched the coal,
But all you lived on was the light that fails.
I would have muscled in with bone-and-roll,
But all your victuals came from fagged-out quails.
You trundle on and fossick out your goal.
But as for me, I'm through. I've furled my sails.'

His LEM is waiting at the station
To take him to the moutains of the moon.
On board he hears the countdown with elation,
Is horrified to see his mother swoon
And turn into a dim, distant relation.
He sees his world become a macaroon.
'Quite a small step for our civilisation —
Not at all bad for a legless baboon.'

We track the craft with cynical defiance,
Raising our damp proboscises to sniff
At such a flight, such pitiful reliance
Upon the parabolic hippogriff.
The module vanishes. Blinded by science.
We camp along the edges of the cliff.
Who slip between the sheets at night with giants
Will wake to pillow dew and morning stiff.

Under the glass dome all its feathers wilt.
The kingfisher grows tetchy and looks bored.
Beneath the cliffs the dawn spreads miles of silt
And lug-worm castings where the breakers roared
Last night. The tattooed man beneath his quilt
Fondles his tattooed limbs. The cutter's hoard
Supports his head, locked in its custom-built
Toledo–steel–bound chest. He grasps his sword.

All fast asleep. The kingfisher and I
Exchange a soulful look, thinking of Home.
The shovellers home shrieking through the sky.
The kingfisher coughs twice and shakes its comb.
'Don't bite your nails so!' But the bird is sly,
Stares at the red horizon where the foam
Curls like a lip, and weeps: 'Ah, let us fly!'
Nettled, I raise my arm — and break the dome.


# THE WILD ONES

Here come the capybaras on their bikes.
They swerve into the friendly, leafy square
Knocking the angwantibos off their trikes,
Giving the old-age coypus a bad scare.
They specialise in nasty, lightning strikes.
They leave the banks and grocers' shops quite bare,
Then swagger through the bardoors for a shot
Of anything the barman hasn't got.

They spoil the friendly rodent rodeos
By rustling the grazing flocks of mice.
They wear enormous jackboots on their toes.
Insulted by a comment, in a trice
They whip their switchblades out beneath your nose.
Their favourite food is elephant and rice.
Their personal appearance is revolting
Their fur is never brushed and always moulting.

And in the evening when the sun goes down
They take the comely women on their backs
And ride for several furlongs out of town
Along the muddy roads and mountain tracks,
Wearing a grim and terrifying frown.
Months later, all the females have attacks
And call the coypu doctors to their beds.
What's born has dreadful capybara heads.

# WIND

This is the wind, the wind in a field of corn.
Great crowds are fleeing from a major disaster
Down the long valleys, the green swaying wadis,
Down through the beautiful catastrophe of wind.

Families, tribes, nations and their livestock
Have heard something, seen something. An expectation
Or a gigantic misunderstanding has swept over the hilltop
Bending the ear of the hedgerow with stories of fire and sword.

I saw a thousand years pass in two seconds.
Land was lost, languages rose and divided.
This lord went east and found safety.
His brother sought Africa and a dish of aloes.

Centuries, minutes later, one might ask
How the hilt of a sword wandered so far from the smithy.
And somewhere they will sing: 'Like chaff we were borne
In the wind.' This is the wind in a field of corn.


# THE SONG THAT SOUNDS LIKE THIS
*To Philip Dennis*

Have you not heard the song
The Song That Sounds Like This
When skies are overcast and looks grow long
And Radio Three
Is all your tea-time company.
The last of the first infusion comes so strong
The apostle spoon wakes up
And clambers from the cup.
Have you not heard it? Have you not heard the song —
Antithesis of bliss —
The Song That Sounds Like This!

Have you not heard them sing
Those songs that sound like these
When yearning for the telephone to ring.
The sky is dark.
The dogs have gone to foul the park.

The first of the next infusion tastes like string.
   Oh melancholy sound.
   All the apostle spoons have drowned.
Have you not heard them, have you not heard them sing —
   No more, oh please,
   Oh give us no more songs,
Oh give us no more Songs That Sound Like These!

# TOM PAULIN

## THE HARBOUR IN THE EVENING

The bereaved years, they've settled to this
Bay-windowed guest house by the harbour wall.
Each of us loved a man who died,
Then learnt how to be old and seem cheerful.
I think of being young, in the coastguard station.
Those cement cottages with the washing
Swaying in the sea wind. What can she see,
The girl I talk to? Victorian childhoods
Where little stick figures go flickering
Along the roads? Such eagerness that used to be.
A butcher's shop, a boarding house, the dead
Are smiling from the windows there.
So many names, faces, and used things.
Dry calico, the smell of cedar wood . . .
I keep them in a drowsy kind of wisdom.
I have my drawer of rings and photographs.

The waves rustle on the beach like starched silk.
And girls come walking down a staircase
Into a wide room where lamps are burning.
Love was a danger and then children.
At sunset, when I saw the white beacon
On the quay, I felt a tear starting.
But I was happy like a woman who opens a door
And hears music. It was your face I saw.
I heard your voice, its gentleness.
And I stared over the water at another coast,
An old woman in a sleep of voices.

## WHERE ART IS A MIDWIFE

In the third decade of March,
A Tuesday in the town of Z —

The censors are on day-release.
They must learn about literature.

There are things called ironies,
Also symbols, which carry meaning.

The types of ambiguity
Are as numerous as the enemies

Of the state. Formal and bourgeois,
Sonnets sing of the old order,

Its lost gardens where white ladies
Are served wine in the subtle shade.

This poem about a bear
Is not a poem about a bear.

It might be termed a satire
On a loyal friend. Do I need

To spell it out? Is it possible
That none of you can understand?


# THE GARDEN OF SELF-DELIGHT

In that garden to the south
the civil gods are ranged
like statues in a maze
of vines and bay leaves.

The fountain grows a dance
of dreaming surfaces —
none of my slow guesses
will tell how deep they are.

And the men who walk the paths
murmur and hold hands
for they are special friends
who like a fragrant verse.

The taut women pass them by,
virgins of the moon
drifting through the cool
evening in their gowns.

This is a playful place,
though I view it from a bruised
shore that is dark blue
and cold and rigorous.

How can I understand
these fine and gracious beings
who pass me by and sing
lightly to each other?

Saying art is for itself
and prays to mirrors in the sand,
its own mirros of burnt sand
where the smooth forms look pure.

So tell me there's no law,
and all of life is like a wine
that settles and grows ripe
till it dances on the tongue.


# A LYRIC AFTERWARDS

There was a taut dryness all that summer
and you sat each day in the hot garden
until those uniformed comedians
filled the street with their big white ambulance,
fetching you and bringing you back to me.

Far from the sea of ourselves we waited
and prayed for the tight blue silence to give.
In your absence I climbed to a square room
where there were dried flowers, folders of sonnets
and crossword puzzles: call them musical

snuffboxes or mannered anachronisms,
they were all too uselessly intricate,
caskets of the dead spirit. Their bitter
constraints and formal pleasures were a style
of being perfect in despair; they spoke

with the vicious trapped crying of a wren.
But that is changed now, and when I see you

walking by the river, a step from me,
there is this great kindness everywhere:
now in the grace of the world and always.


## UNDER CREON

Rhododendrons growing wild below a mountain
and no long high wall or trees either;
a humped road, bone-dry, with no one —
passing one lough and then another
where water-lilies glazed, primed like traps.

A neapish hour, I searched out gaps
in that imperial shrub: a free voice sang
dissenting green, and syllables spoke
holm oaks by a salt shore, their dark tangs
glistening like Nisus in a night attack.

The daylight gods were never in this place
and I had pressed beyond my usual dusk
to find a cadence for the dead: McCracken,
Hope, the northern starlight, a death mask
and the levelled grave that Biggar traced;

like an epic arming in an olive grove
this was a stringent grief and a form of love.
Maybe one day I'll get the hang of it
and find joy, not justice, in a snapped connection,
that Jacobin oath on the black mountain.


## BLACK BREAD
*for Ann Pasternak Slater*

Splitting birches, spiky thicket, kinship —
this is the passionate, the phonic surface
I can take only on trust, like a character
translated to a short story whose huge language
he doesn't know. So we break black bread
in the provinces and can't be certain
what it is we're missing, or what sacrament

this might be, the loaf wrapped in a shirt–tail
like a prisoner's secret or a caked ikon,
that is sour and good, and has crossed over versts,
kilometres, miles. It's those journeys
tholed under the salt stars, in the eager wind
that starves sentries and students in their long coats.
Claudius is on the phone, hear that hard
accent scraping its boots on the threshold,
his thick acid voice in your uncle's conscience,
*I'd have known better how to defend my friend.*
Bitter! Bitter! Bitter! the wedding-guests chant
in bast sandals, and pickled cucumbers
cry out in a prickly opera and round grains
of coriander stud the desert crust.
It's a lump of northern peat, itself alone,
and kin to the black earth, to shaggy speech;
I'll taste it on my tongue next year in the holy,
freed city of gold and parchment.

## TO THE LINEN HALL

After extremity
art turns social
and it's more than fashion
to voice the word *we*.
The epic yawp
hangs like an echo
of the big bang,
though now we tell children
to shun that original —
primal light, soaked green,
the slob mud
and a salt tang.
There is a ban
on philosophies of blood,
a terse demand
for arts and skills
to be understood,
and a common flow
into the new academy
which rules with a chill,
strenuous and insistent,
enforced formality.

Here we have a form
and a control
that is our own,
and on the stone steps
of that eighteenth-century,
reasoned library
we catch the classic spore
of Gibbon and new *ceps*,
the busts and statues
that might be stored
under the squares.
Our shaping brightness
is a style and discipline
that finds its tongue
in the woody desk-dawns
of fretting scholars
who pray, invisibly,
to taste the true vine
and hum gently
in holy sweetness.

# ANDREW MOTION

## LEAVING BELFAST
*for Craig Raine*

Driving at dusk on the steep road
north to the airport, 'Look back',
you say, 'The finest view of Belfast',
and point, proud of your choice to stay.

How clear the rows of streetlamps show
which way we came. I trace them slope
by slope through marshlands slipping down
to lanes, and find the roofs again,

their stern geographies of punishment
and love where silence deepens under rain.
Each sudden gust of light explains itself
as flames, but neither they, nor even

bombs redoubled on the hills tonight
can quite include me in their fear.
What does remains invisible, is lost
in curt societies whose deaths become

revenge by morning, and whose homes
are nothing more than all they pity most.
I watch the moon above them, filling rooms
with shadow politics, though whether

voices there pronounce me an intruder,
traitor, or a friend, I leave them now
as much a stranger as I came, and turn
to listen in the twilight for their griefs,

but hear instead the promise of conclusion
fading fast towards me through these miles
of stubborn gorse, until it disappears
at last in darkness, out beyond the coast.

# NO NEWS FROM THE OLD COUNTRY

I

Well, how do they look, the hills of Vermont,
now that you're back? Smaller? And closer the house?
In thirty years it isn't the weather that's changed them,
but you, contracting the past by turning away.

Restore it now. England's dependable winters
were never enough, but there, watching the hills
repeat their promise of danger, you're home
on original ground. Let it build back —

fresh shadows have pressed across your room,
and further, the forest you never explored
has flooded new valleys. O let it build back,
not as explicable, thin enchantment,

but as a place in extremity: all its rivers
and broken roads defining a wilderness
where you relearn your love of chances,
and, as I write, even by pushing out

through your gate towards the trees
to search for kindling, are suddenly lost
from sight in a flutter of snow from a bough,
and found in the dark, risking another world.

II

So it goes on; so I, in the old country
live off borrowed adventures. Since you left here
nothing has changed to disturb its complacent stillness;
or rather, there's only your absence starting again

each day, unreal and substantial at once,
like a hole in the air. But otherwise
there are the same identical views, which never
develop or move: the park, the thicket of steeples,

and even the river which carries down news
from miles inland is frozen across.
The rubbish of summer sealed in ice!
So much for different worlds. Where are you now?

High up in the woods, alone? Here there's only
the city's floodlit, familiar dark
fading towards you as England turns out of the sun.
O love, how did it start, this suburban safety,

this living on rumours of action? And now,
when will it end, pretending a possible happiness
somewhere else, another beginning, a river
tapped at its first, immaculate source?

# A DYING RACE

The less I visit, the more I think
myself back to your elegant house
I grew up in. The drive uncurled
through swaying chestnuts discovers
it standing four square, white-
washed unnaturally clear,
as if it were shown me by lightning.

It's always the place I see,
not you. You're somewhere outside,
waving goodbye where I left you
a decade ago. I've even lost sight
of losing you now; all I can find
are the mossy steps you stood on
— a visible loneliness.

I'm living four counties away, and still
I think of you driving south each night
to the ward where your wife
is living. How long will it last?
You've made that journey six years
already, taking comparative happinesses
like a present, to please her.

I can remember the fields you pass,
the derelict pill-boxes squatting
in shining plough. If I was still there,
watching your hand push back
the hair from her desperate face,
I might have discovered by now the way
love looks, its harrowing clarity.

# ANNE FRANK HUIS

Even now, after twice her lifetime of grief
and anger in the very place, whoever comes
to climb these narrow stairs, discovers how
the bookcase slides aside, then walks through
shadow into sunlit rooms, can never help

but break her secrecy again. Just listening
is a kind of guilt: the Westerkirk repeats
itself outside, as if all time worked round
towards her fear, and made each stroke
die down on guarded streets. Imagine it —

three years of whispering and loneliness
and plotting, day by day, the Allied line
in Europe with a yellow chalk. What hope
she had for ordinary love and interest
survives her here, displayed above the bed

as pictures of her family; some actors;
fashions chosen by Princess Elizabeth.
And those who stoop to see them find
not only patience missing its reward,
but one enduring wish for chances

like my own: to leave as simply
as I do, and walk at ease
up dusty tree-lined avenues, or watch
a silent barge come clear of bridges
settling their reflections in the blue canal.

# ONE LIFE

Up country, her husband is working late
on a high cool veranda. His radio plays
World Service News, but he does not listen,
and does not notice how moonlight fills
the plain below, with its ridge of trees
and shallow river twisting to Lagos
a whole night's journey south. What holds

him instead are these prizes that patience
and stealthy love have caught: *papilio
dardanus* — each with the blacks and whites
of simple absolutes he cannot match.

She understands nothing of this.
Away in her distant room, she lies
too sick to see the bar-sign steadily print
its purple letters over and over her wall.
Too tired to care when the silence breaks
and this stranger, her friend, leans smiling
above the bed. There is just one implausible
thought that haunts her as clear and perfect
as ever — the delicate pottery bowl she left
forgotten at home, still loaded with apples
and pears she knows by their English names.


# HUMAN GEOGRAPHY

Hardly believing it, we left each other
in the hot gale of the underground — you
to the time you could not give up, and I
to my family holidays lolling in parched
Ionian heat: olive groves, tortuous roads
and vodka precisely at six.

I write on the terrace now, reliving it all.
Grandfather sits as he does each day
watching the lazy sea pucker and smooth,
with his eyes vague and his back set
to the island and Europe behind it. 'Ruined',
he says. 'A class and manners unknown to me'.

What he resents is you. And I think of you
changing for sleep two hours away
in that rented room, with your bare spine
bowed as you shrug your nightshirt on.
'The war'. He bends towards me again,
amused to discover his life is history.

'Changed it all. To think. The Kaiser, here . . .'
Then gestures clumsily over the bay, half drunk

and almost asleep, to show the Achilleon squaring
its massive shadow downhill. Tall lights appear,
CASINO in pink, and car by car the gamblers
gather at tables where soldiers signalled

'Im Western Nichts Neues' to sentries, changing
the guard on their flagship a mile below.
I picture roulette exactly — a ball flicked
round on the wheel, rested, then thrown once more —
with nothing to say. Grandfather shuffles inside.
The sunset thins to a smear of darkening gold.

# FRANK KUPPNER

## SVENSK RAPSODI
*44 Comments on a little book of pictures of the same name*


1.
Since buying this book more or less for nothing slightly over a year
    ago,
I have lost it at least twice, and twice found it,
(At no time ever having missed its presence),
When I was actually looking for something else.


2.
Inside the front cover was already written,
"To Alison from Barbro; Christmas 1965:
Merry Christmas and Happy New Year" (in Swedish);
Oh my coevals, I too received mail that week.


3.
Inscribed in a youthful hand, a mere two lines,
When I too was a child; but I have grown up,
And have covered their ageing gift with an adult scribble,
While their own hands form their adult scribbles elsewhere.


4.
Had it cost more than peanuts, I would never have bought it;
It is, to be sure, not a particularly good book;
The photographic views are not particularly impressive;
If my poems fail, then at least they are appropriate.


5. COVER SCENE
Before a representatively picturesque house,
Two identically gauche young girls try to pose,
Each holding one handle of a large wicker basket;
In a nearby city, their parents strike each other.


6. SPRING
How many Swedish trees have never been touched?
How many, for that matter, have been touched only once:
By a shambling hunter, with a quaintly low forehead,
Or the girl lost for an hour from her group of hikers.

### 7. SUMMER
Oh yes, I have heard about these quiet chalets;
These chalets hidden in the green-gold light of trees,
Apparently deserted, even in the fullness of summer;
I wish I had brought my binoculars along.

### 8. AUTUMN
The near trees are gold; the trees behind them green;
The yellow crops are murmuring of granaries;
As a sole cloud swims voluptuously in the sky,
I can hear a blonde whispering in the forest.

### 9. WINTER
I stare at a picture of timber in a snowy field;
I look again at this picture of logs in the snow;
But the neck of the girl beside me this afternoon,
In the sun-drenched garden, slowly beginning to glisten.

### 10.
This view reminds me, with uncanny exactness,
Of a scene I regularly glimpse from the train
On trips down to my parents' home on the coast;
Of course, that year they still were living in the city.

### 11. BEECH WOOD IN SCANIA
Oho, beechtrees with your soft golden carpet;
I am not the idiot you take me for;
Which of you has been kissed by someone who has seen me?
Come on; I know there must be at least *one* of you.

### 12.
Oho, beechtrees with your soft golden carpet;
I am not the idiot you take me for;
Behind which of you are the little blondes hiding?
Step aside, I pray you — a sudden step right or left.

### 13. KULLEN, SCANIA
The sea laps around some cold, glistering stones;
Beyond them lies a beach of dry grey warm stones;
And, in the difference between these two types of stone,
Surely Life itself is contained, or Death, or something.

14. SKREASTRAND
And here we have an extremely rare species:
Sprawled or sitting in this well-sheltered beach,
1960's sunbathers who talk in Swedish;
Let us look out tentatively from behind this grassy dune.


15.
Before a representatively picturesque house,
Two identically gauche young girls try to pose,
Each holding one handle of a large wicker basket;
I suspect there is nothing in the large wicker basket.


16. GOTHENBURG
I see nothing extraordinary about those ships;
I see nothing extraordinary about those fixed cranes;
They seem just as improbable as all cranes do;
Is something happening in that small block of waterfront flats?


17.
A blade of grass reaches up above the metal railway-track;
Over it towers a huge stone-cutter at work;
The blue length of his trouser-leg is framed by some hard-edged
    rocks;
That other blue strip beyond him may be the sea.


18. SMÖGEN
The patches of moss scattered over the rocks
Are far less neat than the row of fishermen's houses,
But somehow the eye travels more readily to them;
Except for some rock-face where the thirteenth house ought to be.


19.
Floating placidly down the green canal,
It was only on the 103rd morning,
When still the destination had not been reached,
That the first whispers began to be heard on board.


20. ALVARET
On the thin, narrow, unimportant island a gate is shut;
If it were to be opened in the next ten seconds,
A certain nearby star would obliterate;
But fortunately, the little island seems deserted.

21.
Some of those trees are in one country, and others in another;
Is it a branch of the river that is the actual border?
Yet again, Nature shows up a human inadequacy;
Actually, I find Nature intensely irritating sometimes.


22. MARIEFRED
If I can say something about this photograph,
I will have commented on all the pictures in the book;
A pleasant little scene, with reflections and boats,
Reflections and boats; there must be something else.


23. GOTLAND
Ever since that day in the fourteenth century,
Or possibly in the fifteenth century,
When marauding Greeks rolled kegs up the tree-lined pathway,
The old Gotlandish church has never been convincingly quiet.


24.
Before a representatively picturesque house,
Two identically gauche young girls try to pose,
Each holding one handle of a large wicker basket;
Was that not the year I went to Italy?


25. VISBY
The crenellated tower cuts across the line of the sea;
An utterly placid, extensive, deep blue sea;
The old man strolls beside the city walls,
On his way home to cook a meal of fish.


26. KORNHAMNSTORG
It seems to be the rule with continental squares,
That one small blue car is always parked unaccompanied;
To give more picturesqueness to the tourists' photographs,
And raise a question in their minds twenty years later.


27. NYBROPLAN
How I love those pictures of important buildings,
With slices of unimportant buildings at their side,
With a line of fascinating, accidental windows;
Open or closed; clean or dirty; half-open.

28. STOCKHOLM
Amid profound cheering, the important personage steps ashore;
A man who has fallen out of an aeroplane
Lands with a sickening thud on the parade beside him;
He defuses the situation with a witty remark.


29. STOCKHOLM
The important personage steps ashore amid profound cheering;
A man who has fallen out of a helicopter
Lands with a sickening thud on the parade beside her;
The Queen ignores it, with typical sang froid.


30. SANDHAMN
A graceful corps-de-ballet of sailing-boats
Tosses beside a mixture of wood and green,
Placidly accepting summer and calmness;
But which does not contain past shrieks of terror?


31. SIGTUNA
Six ducks float placidly in a small pond,
Quite unperturbed that this is all that remains
Of what was once known as the Atlantic Ocean;
Fifteen million duck-hunters crawl towards them.


32.
Ten minutes of respite among the falls of rain;
They hurry along the squelching grassy path;
The farm-door swings open before they reach the wood;
They look up to the clouds, and then back to the door.


33. VÄRMLAND
The country-house is utterly symmetrical;
It is obviously occupied by twins;
At the opposite end of the flawless garden pool,
A stone nymph turns her head away in disgust.


34.
Before a representatively picturesque house,
Two identically gauche young girls try to pose,
Each holding one handle of a large wicker basket;
As yet, one cannot see traces of madness in her features.

### 35. LEKSAND

In an interesting relic of their pre-Christian ceremonies,
The parson rows out to the middle of the lake,
Throws the bride and groom into the pellucid water,
And hurries to try to set their new house on fire.

### 36. JÄMTLAND

A tiny snatch of road can be seen in the foreground;
A few small stones are visible where they are;
1964, eh?
I was in Germany the year after that.

### 37. SILLRE

For all the world like a northern branch of the Rhine,
But without a single castle along its banks;
Baffled minstrels gazing about themselves, lost,
Are a sight only slightly less common than reindeer.

### 38. SANDSLÅN

The lake has been entirely covered by logs;
More and more spill out of the attendant rivers,
Filling the lake and stretching into the sea;
Reports soon come in of cities being built.

### 39. LÖVÅNGER

I have never seen such utterly convincing weeds,
Not since the over-extended days of childhood,
When, for some reason, one spends so much time among weeds;
Insects too are quintessentially childish.

### 40. JOKKMOKK

Then, after the 97,000th pine forest,
It is not yet another wide waterfall,
But the actual ocean which stretches out in front of us;
And so we went back to the town, to search for elbows.

### 41.

A sea of useful stones lies about the mineworks:
That one there will take part in a Swedish fireplace;
That one there will take part in a Chilean fireplace;
That one there will be trodden beneath the mud.

42.
A sea of useful stones lies about the mineworks,
And many of them will be kissed by happy blondes;
Of course, they lie there as supine as any others;
But do not believe there is no envy in stones.

43. VASSIJAURE
The problem with this place is that there are no Chinese here;
Snow, space, and pine-trees are glorious, but not enough;
Basically, what one wants is almond-shaped eyes
That light up in anger as a snowball narrowly misses them.

44.
Before a representatively picturesque house,
Two identically gauche young girls are trying to pose,
Each holding one handle of a large wicker basket;
In nearby towns, their parents flex their knee-joints.

# ALISON BRACKENBURY

## DERBY DAY: AN EXHIBITION

The great Stubbs' picture of the great Eclipse
Hangs in the corner it defies,
Effortless. The great are luminous.
Orbed flanks shine solid, amber, having won.
A gold-red horse called Hermit won, and broke
The wild Earl of Hastings, who had flung
Woods and fields against. What can Eclipse
Comfort those eclipsed, who never won?

The young Fred Archer with a boy's sad face,
Shot himself, sick dizzy on the edge.
He won six flaring Derbys. Not that one
In which a woman sprang beneath the rail.
In thudding dark, pain tore all colours; died.

And yet a brilliant day. Do not mistake:
That which we do best kills us. Horse and man
Amber in the mist of downs, sea-shore,
The spring of wave, glow greatly. They survive

## KINGDOMS

Gold, edged with green, the peacock's eyes
Ducked and shimmered past my head
To see the young Athenians
who could not leap the bull, lie dead.
Their ended screams still twist my sleep
become the staircase where I run,
of alabaster pale as milk
in courtyards where the black bull shone
his high horns lashed with reddened silk.

Black, pierced with grey, prick morning's leaves,
where all the headdresses lie dark
crushed in rough volcano ash;
where now we sleep in shelters, cracks
in painted stones: in fear I brush
for morning's sticks through the deep wood.

A young black bull they would have found
with net, gold rope for sacrifice
Stirs through the thicket: I am caught
only in his drowsing eyes:
a smudge of mist. He rubs the grey
smooth trunk; blinks sleep, walks slow away

For pomp and cold twigs crackle: fade.
In a still space I am drawn.
Fire, be moth-wing, grey and gold,
Bull and dancer: ash and dawn.


## 'YESTERDAY VIVALDI VISITED ME; AND SOLD ME SOME VERY EXPENSIVE CONCERTOS'

He had only one tune.
And that
a thin finger on pulses:
of spring and the frost,
                              the quick turn of girls' eyes
a tune

to hold against darkness,
to fret
for trumpet, for lute
for flutes; violins
to silver the shabbiness
of many towns
the fool's bowl, the court coat,
a tune he would give:
without sorrow or freedom
again, again
                there is only one tune.

Sell it dearly to live.

# INTIMATES

You lived too near the ghosts. For they were kind
dry, warm as snakes you never feared.
Speak now of love to men whose eyes
are moist and cold,
unkind as the true world.

For you are woken now by evening's rain
(a snake would shiver, slip into the dark)
are startled as it smashes on hot land.
The sky-light leaks. Rain pricks against your wrist ––
Strange fingers slip the gold ring from your hand.

# THE HOUSE

It was the house of childhood, the house of the dark wood,
four-square and safe, it was the second house
at least, to bear its name. The first was burnt: was charred
foundations, hidden by a timber yard.

I knew this in my dream: the house was same
and solid. All its yews, church trees, were strong
red wood of generations. As we came
out in the dusk sight heaved, house, orchard, gone.
Cold in the trembling grass we shivered there.
On open hillside, to the first stars' stare

I watched dark, unsurprised. I could remember
the bombers roaring low above the trees
to reach their high 'drome, though the war was done.
The house had strained and crumbled.
                              there is only
          the old magic, forced out in new ways.
Hard through the dream's cold spring I raised
My house again. My bones and my heart ache
In every joist. The altered rooms are filled
With lovely light: the only house
Which kills in falling, which you must rebuild —

          In new wood boxes, apples there
All winter breathe out sweetness, in cold air.

# ROBERT BRACKENBURY

Ancestors are not in our blood, but our heads:
we make history.
Therefore I claim
you, from dark folds of Lincolnshire
who share my name
and died two hundred years ago
you, man, remembered there
for doing good: lost, strange and sharp you rise
like smoke: because it was your will
all letters, papers, perish when you died.

Who burnt them? Wife or daughter, yawning maid
poked down the struggling blackness in the grate
or walked slow, to the place where leaves were burnt,
the white air, winter's. Slips of ash
trembled on the great blue cabbage leaves:
O frozen sea.

Why Robert, did
you hate the cant of epitaph so much?
leave action to be nothing but itself:
the child who walked straight-legged, the man,
whose house no longer smoked with rain, and yet
(soft scent of grass in other men's archives)
your name, to linger; did you trust
that when all shelves, all studies fell to ash
your kindness still might haunt our wilderness
a hand that plucks at us, a stubborn leaf
twitching before rain

                    or did despair
turn: whisper there how you were young
to burn and change your world: not enough done,
from that you turned

to silence and a shadowed wall; unkind
to family, to wife, and to that maid:

Who buried you, for love, in Christian ground.

I think that you had ceased to trust in knowledge.
You did not want the detail of your life

wrapped round us like a swaddling cloth; passed, known,
to shadow over us like a great tree.
The crumbling, merging soil, the high rooks
cawing out the black spring are for you;
now we must speak and act: make day alone.

In one thing I'll be resolute as you.
In white day in the thawing grass I'll burn
one letter, then the bundles; stare
at the cracked silvering of walnut bark:
and see what, in that grace? Not you,
your eyes of frozen dark.
Perhaps the combed light of the counterpane,
the hot breath, that is action, the mist closing

huddled in cloth:

                   turned eyes, the smoke's sharp glow:

snatch back the half-charred letter. In the icy
blue, wasted leaves watch silent the unmaking
flames crumble white

too like a God forsaking
the heart of ash.

And though I made you, though
I should ask nothing of you,
I will turn against you, bitter
as the girl's mouth in the garden
tasting winter, ashes: glow
of fire that cannot warm us
or ever quite betray,
smoke that twists the cold hand
         in shapes I do not know.

# AN ORANGE OF CLOVES

Clove-scent: the dark room where the lovers lie
A closet smelling both of must and musk,
Which makes the head faint: rawer and more old
Than pale-flowered stocks which scent the dusk.

Cavern of dark I entered first: I thought
I have danced here, and to a golden lute.
Branched velvet, rushes, gallows in the sunlight —

sense shudders till it glimpses in a space
The great sharp-scented tree, its flowers, its fruit
All of a season, beating in the rain;
The orange, cloves cross-cleft; and past the pain,
a dark tree fading, seeding in each face.

# FOUR POEMS

## I

Strange sea: sudden sea: no thing can be the same.
I think of snowdrops and lit hedgerows which
may never have been there.
What lay in that drink that we should stare,
the birds shout salt and harsh; black ways
gape between the water and your eyes?
I burn and my bones melt to gold.
And as I grip your hard wrist and we rise
I understand how our love lies:

not in waves' green light but light's great cold

## II

By the king's tree I walked afraid.
You spoke your riddles tenderly:

Is not the moon's cold rising made
To lure the salt sea from the land?

Is not the horse which bolts with you
Gentle in stall, to brush your hand

And the amazing cherry tree
Rooted in possibility?

Silence. The dazzling boughs above
dance white belief I dare not prove.

## III

I am the maid who slept with you
To cheat you on your wedding night.
Mine is the mouth that parts on you
questing, till the birds cry light.
You the dark shape on the cliff,
my dreaded lord, my lovely man
No maid or woman in the world
can hate or take you as I can.
My feet crush thyme. The fluid lark
Fuses your voices, Tristan, Mark.

## IV

It could go on for ever so; the giving
As the sea melts into the autumn haze
I could wear out my weariness with love
Not knowing yet which shadow cools my days
Black king; a young man on a sunlit deck.
Fearing the wrecks where seas in winter break
I walk the garden's walks alone and plant
Two autumn crocuses the tall winds shake
To shivered blue of eyes. You wrote to me
We might at least 'preserve intensity'.
Not quite Isolde; but the crocus lit
to stranger flame. Through fear and work's ache we
read the dark's story; risk; since one forgot
to change the heavy sails from black to white
another died. As in an older story
the grieved man leapt from cliffs, crashed down in light.
The lark lifts struggling but she frees her voice.
Our business is avoiding tragedy.
My double flower: give me no choice
Between black ships and empty sea.

# MEDINE IN TURKEY

'Today' said Hassan — through a mouthful of honey —
'A girl will come who speaks French.' There came
A girl with straight brown hair, her eyes
Flecked with gold, a stiller honey.
Her French was pure and soft. Her name
Was Medine. Her paid study
Ended when her father died.
'Maintenant — j'aide ma mere. Je lis.'

'Je lis Freud,' she ventured, bare feet firm
On the rug's blurred leaves. She lived next door.
Each house leads to a tiny yard
With a dusty tree; white chickens squirm
In favourite hollows. She never saw
France; she sat, this grave brown child
Ten years younger than myself, unmarried
Alight, in their cool best room. She smiled.

There is no answer. Scholarships?
France, too, has hot bored villages
With girls who read all afternoon.
The arranged husband, or their child's care
Will not close up that watchful face
Flecked by lace curtains, endless sun;
Unmoved, she listens for the place
Where the book closes, where the footsteps run.

# CASTLE

There are lilies in the lake, the lilies of still water
Which part for nodding ducks and close again.
I cannot see my face, they are so close,
Half-opened only, swayed, red stem to stem;
I cross the trembling bridge. Held in the other
Bank, an arch of broken stone pipes gapes
Five silted throats from which no waters fall.
My eye's edge sees — but that would be too strange —
White open mouths of orchids on a wall.

Around the clock is painted a blue heaven
On which the sun's great cycle gilds, and sings.
I cross the yard, bare even of a cat,
Or outstretched dog; or stir of pigeon's wings.
The arches of the yard are white and even
The brass knob of the door is smudged by hands
And I am slower, heavy as the clouds
Which move across the upper sky in pairs,
Now I have reached my certain journey's end
Turning the corner, climbing the closed stairs.

The window is set open and the door
Was never locked. The carpet, once complete
With hunting dogs, tall pairs of gold-chained birds
Is worn down to dark thread, by other feet.
My foot brushes a plate left on the floor
With the dark skins of fruit; fresh apricots
Whose bloom is gone: whose scent would still hang there
If the room were shuttered, closed and not
Open to this sudden cool of air.

I must come here. I must come, many times
Though there is nothing more that I can see
Inside the room or all its passageways
Where small sounds run, too far ahead of me;
No order, day or night, disturbs the chimes.
Yet I may see — if once, I do not watch —
The glint if the stone roof in dark, the moth
Flown before I touch it. I may catch
A hidden breath; the fluttered, warm, black cloth.


# MARCH NIGHT

The road streams, to the moon. The sky
Is green and solid, lapped by light
The stars are buds, leaf-furled and white

The children clatter out of dark
Pushing down the stable cart.
'Don't crash it, like you did last night!'

My horse licks out my feeding hand
Stares at the upturned cart, diverted:
The slow moon climbs, behind his head.

As the spilled children pause for breath
Above the broken bread and apples,
Across the sudden fields, sound bells.

I never knew bells which have been
Tumbled, mad, and very sweet
Cast seed so, through the sky's cracked green.


# TREES

We are past the Christmas trees, in their wide windows
hung with lights, like fruit. They shine all day.
We have watched the fields, where the moon is rising:
smudged, solemn mouth. Above us, white stars grow:
huge and bare, spread over earth:
a tree of light, a tree of snow.

# MICHAEL HOFMANN

## NIGHTS IN THE IRON HOTEL

Our beds are at a hospital distance.
I push them together. Straw matting on
the walls produces a Palm Beach effect:

long drinks made with rum in tropical bars.
The position of mirror and wardrobe
recalls a room I once lived in happily.

Our feelings are shorter and faster now.
You confess a new infidelity. This time,
a trombone player. His tender mercies . . .

All night, we talk about separating.
The radio wakes us with its muzak.
In a sinister way, you call it lulling.

We are fascinated by our own anaesthesia,
our inability to function. Sex is a luxury,
an export of healthy physical economies.

The TV stays switched on all the time.
Dizzying social realism for the drunks.
A gymnast swings like a hooked fish.

## BOYS' OWN

A parting slightly off-centre, like Oscar Wilde's,
his fat mouth, and the same bulky appearance.
Your hair was pomaded, an immaculate wet-look,
sculpted and old-fashioned in these blow-dry times.
The dull grain of wood on polished furniture.
— Everyone has an inspiring English teacher
somewhere behind them, and you were ours. We argued
about you: that your smell was not sweet after-shave,
but the presbyterian rigours of cold water —

on your porous face and soft, womanish hands . . . ?
The public-school teacher had to be versatile —
if not the genuine Renaissance article, then at least
a modern pentathlete — and so you appeared to us
in as many guises as an Action Man: for lessons,
with a gown over one of your heavy three-piece suits;
wearing khaki for Corps on Wednesday afternoons;
as a soccer referee in a satanic black tracksuit;
in baggy but respectable corduroys on holidays . . .

Morning coffee was followed by pre-prandial sherry
after only the shortest of intervals. The empties,
screw-tops, stood in boxes outside your door.
You drank early, copiously, and every day —
though it hardly crossed our minds. Given the chance,
we would have done too . . . It was 'civilised',
and that was what you were about. Sweet and sour sherry,
lager on warm afternoons, the pathos of sparkling wine
for occasions. 'It's actually quite like champagne . . .'

Just as an extension-lead went from your gramophone
to its little brother, a 'stereophonic' loudspeaker —
Ferguson Major and Minor. . . With one hand in your pocket,
leaning back in your swivelling chair, you conducted
your own records, legs double-crossed like Joyce's.
— Among all those other self-perpetuating oddball
bachelors, how could we fail to understand you?
Your military discipline and vintage appearance,
the sublimation of your Anglicanism, your drinking . . .

We only waited for that moment at the end of a class,
when, exhausted by intellectual inquiry, you took off
your glasses and rubbed away your tiny blue eyes . . .
All of love and death can be found in books;
you would have agreed. At one of your gatherings,
someone found a pubic hair in your sheepskin rug . . .
Years later, there was a scandal, an ultimatum,
and you threw yourself under the wheels of a train —
the severe way Tolstoy chose for Anna Karenina.

# MYOPIA IN RUPERT BROOKE COUNTRY

Birds, feathers, a few leaves, flakes of soot —
things start to fall. The stubble has been burned,
and the fields are striped in black and gold.
Elsewhere, the hay is still drying on long racks:
bulky men prancing about on slender hooves,
unconvincing as pantomime cattle . . . A hedgehog
lies rolled over on its side like a broken castor.
Abandoned in one corner is a caravan that has
not been on holiday all year. Forever England . . .
A hot-air balloon sinks towards the horizon —
the amateur spirit or an advertising gimmick?
Quickly flames light it up, the primitive roar
of a kitchen geyser, and its calcified heart
gives a little skip, then slides down like tears.

# ECLOGUE

Industry undressing in front of Agriculture —
not a pretty sight. The subject for one
of those allegorical Victorian sculptures.
An energetic mismatch. But Pluto's hell–holes
terminate in or around the flower-meadows
and orchards of Proserpine. Ceres' poor daughter
is whisked away by the top-hatted manufacturer
on his iron horse . . . Brick huts in the fields,
barred mine-entrances from the last century,
narrow–gauge railways, powdery cement–factories.
A quarry is an inverted cathedral: witchcraft,
a steeple of air sharpened and buried in the ground.
— All around these dangerous sites, sheep graze,
horned and bleating like eminent Victorians.

# 1967–1971
*for R. H.*

I lived in an L-shaped room, my chair was
almost directly behind the door, so that,
when I was sitting in it, I was virtually
the last thing in the whole room to be seen.
visitors would have to describe a small
circle in order to face me, crouching
on my chair with a book. early one evening
I read most of *David Copperfield*, put it
down for supper, and never finished it.
sometimes, out of nostalgia, I would read
the stories in a children's encyclopaedia,
flicking past the hundreds of pages of
science and travel and other matters
that separated these islands of fiction.
it was the time I was interested in art,
even in abstract painting. my red jumper
and my blue trousers were my favourite
clothes; and least my brown trousers and
lemon-yellow pullover. my last beating
took place then as well, just before lunch.
I had thoughts of resistance, but decided
to let it go; it was somehow understood
that this would be the last time.


# FÜRTH I. WALD
*for Jan and Anja T.*

There are seagulls inland, extensive flooding
and a grey sky. A tractor stalled in midfield
between two goals. Mammoth sawmills collecting trees
and pulping them for furniture and wallpaper . . .
These strips of towns, with their troubled histories,
they are lost in the woods like Hansel and Gretel.
Counters at peace-conferences, they changed hands
so often, they became indistinguishable, worthless.
Polyglot and juggled like Belgium, each of them keeps
a spare name in the other language to fall back on.
Only their wanton, spawning frontier tells them apart,
an arrogant line of wire in an electric clearing.
(A modern derivative of the civic myth of Thebes:

the oxhide cut into ribbons by cunning estate-agents
and laid end-to-end; so many towns called Cuernavaca . . .)
— At other frontiers, it may be a long tunnel instead,
too long for you to hold your breath. At halfway,
the texture of the concrete changes, and the lights,
but you can't say where it is brighter or safer . . .
Nations are irregular parcels, tight with fear.
But their contents have settled during transport.
*Grenzflucht*. Perimeters that are now deserted and
timid, the dream-wrappings clash with each other.
On one side, the lonely heartless villas of the guards.
Dustbins stored like sandbags outside barrackrooms.
The play of searchlights . . . On the other, *Der Neue
Tag* dawns only twice a week nowadays. With its
Nazi-sounding name and millenarian ideals, still
holding the fort for a dwindling readership . . .


# C. & W.
*for Sara*

Musicians from the cradle . . . Birth, marriage
and death, to the whine of steel guitars.
Rows of petticoats — high kicks at the hoe-down.
You start putting a few words together
for a song, and they turn into a complaint.

I'm a simple man. Living is never easy,
but women are flowers when you can get them.
And they can be mean, or they cheat on you . . .
Her hair was long and black as ravens' wings.
In five minutes, she killed our love with words.

The memory is lethal, I stayed drunk for years.
In this world, misfortunes don't happen singly.
Lightning always strikes at the same spot . . .
My best cowboy shirt was destroyed by fire,
tears have rusted the strings of my guitar.

# THE AUSTRIANS AFTER SADOWA (1866)

They live as well as they can — the irony
of a small people living in a small country
that was once an empire, with its own navy
and foreign policy, administration and style.
In this century of their loss, they have had
more than their share of innovators; dominating
in philosophy, science, psychology, the arts . . .
After the death of power, the lightning of analysis.

# BIOGRAPHICAL NOTES

PETER SCUPHAM was born in Liverpool in 1933, educated at the Perse and Emmanuel College, Cambridge, after National Service. He is married, with three sons and a daughter. Currently he teaches in Hertfordshire and runs, with John Mole, the Mandeville Press, of which he is the proprietor. His books include *The Snowing Globe* (1972), *Prehistories* (1975), *The Hinterland* (1977), *Summer Palaces* (1980) and *Winter Quarters* (1983).

TONY HARRISON was born in Leeds in 1937, educated at Leeds Grammar School and the University of Leeds where he read Classics. He spent four years in Northern Nigeria and a year teaching at Charles University, Prague, served as Poetry Fellow in Newcastle-on-Tyne and in Durham, and in 1969 won awards which enabled him to travel to Cuba, Brazil, Senegal and the Gambia. His first major collection, *The Loiners*, won the Geoffrey Faber Memorial Prize. His translations of classical and French dramatic work and of opera libretti for British and American theatres are numerous. Other poetry publications include *The School of Eloquence* (1978) and *Continuous* (1981).

GILLIAN CLARKE was born in Cardiff in 1937 and has lived in South Wales for most of her life. She works as a part-time lecturer in Gwent College of Art & Design and edits *The Anglo-Welsh Review*. Her publications include *Snow on the Mountains* (1971), *The Sundial* (1978) and *Letter from a Far Country* (1982).

ANDREW WATERMAN was born in London in 1940. Since 1968 he has worked at the New University of Ulster, where he is Senior Lecturer in English. His collections of poetry are *Living Room* (1974), *From the Other Country* (1977), *Over the Wall* (1980) and *Out for the Elements* (1981).

DEREK MAHON was born in Belfast in 1941 and educated at Trinity College, Dublin. He is married, with two children, and lives in London, where he works as a journalist and screenwriter. His work was brought together in *Poems 1962-1978* (1979), which was followed by *The Hunt by Night* (1982).

JEREMY HOOKER was born in Southampton in 1941 and educated at Southampton University. He has been a Lecturer in English at Aberystwyth since 1965. *A View from the Source: selected poems* (1982) drew on four earlier collections.

JEFFREY WAINWRIGHT was born in Stoke-on-Trent in 1944. He read English at Leeds University and now teaches at Manchester Polytechnic;

he has also taught in Wales and America. His book of poems *Heart's Desire* (1978) included material from his Northern House pamphlet *The Important Man*.

DAVID CONSTANTINE was born in 1944 in Salford, Lancashire. He read Modern Languages at Oxford and became a lecturer in English at Durham University. In 1981 he became Fellow of German at Queen's College, Oxford. He has published two books of poems: *A Brightness to Cast Shadows* (1980) and *Watching for Dolphins* (1983).

DICK DAVIS was born in Portsmouth in 1945. After graduating from Cambridge, he worked as a teacher, first in Yorkshire and later abroad. In 1978 he returned from Iran to England and is now a freelance writer. His books of poetry are *In the Distance* (1975) and *Seeing the World* (1980).

CLIVE WILMER was born in Harrogate, Yorkshire, in 1945, but grew up in South London, read English at Cambridge, taught abroad in Italy, and then returned to Cambridge where he now teaches. His books of poetry are *The Dwelling-Place* (1977) and *Devotions* (1982).

ROBERT WELLS was born in Oxford in 1947. After graduating from Cambridge he worked as a forester in Exmoor and later taught in Iran and Italy. He lectured for a time at the University of Leicester and is now working at Oxford on a new translation of Theocritus. He has published one book of poems, *The Winter's Task* (1977).

JOHN ASH was born in Manchester in 1948. He read English at the University of Birmingham, taught for a year in Cyprus, and returned to Manchester. His collections of poetry include *Casino* (1978), *The Bed and Other Poems* (1981) and *The Goodbyes* (1982).

JAMES FENTON was born in Lincoln in 1949 and educated at Oxford. He worked as a journalist in England and abroad, in Indo-China and Germany. He is now theatre critic of the *Sunday Times*. His books include *Terminal Moraine* (1972), *The Memory of War: Poems 1968-1982* (1982) and *Children in Exile* (1983).

TOM PAULIN was born in Leeds in 1949 and brought up in Belfast. He studied at the Universities of Hull and Oxford and is now a Lecturer in English at the University of Nottingham. His collections include *A State of Justice* (1977), *The Strange Museum* (1980) and *Liberty Tree* (1983).

ANDREW MOTION was born in London in 1952 and educated at Oxford. He lectured at the University of Hull and was later editor of *Poetry Review*. He is currently poetry editor at Chatto and Windus. His collections include *The Pleasure Steamers* (1978), *Independence* (1981) and *Secret Narratives* (1983).

FRANK KUPPNER was born in Glasgow in 1952. His first book of poems, *A Bad Day for the Sung Dynasty*, will appear in 1984.

ALISON BRACKENBURY was born in Lincolnshire in 1953. She read English at Oxford. Until recently she worked as a librarian in Gloucestershire. Her first book of poems was *Dreams of Power* (1981). *Breaking Ground*, her second, is due in 1984.

MICHAEL HOFMANN was born in Freiburg, Germany, in 1957, but grew up mostly in England. He read English at Cambridge. His first collection of poems is *Nights in the Iron Hotel* (1983).

# ACKNOWLEDGEMENTS

Thanks are due to the following poets and publishers for permission to print or re-print poems and excerpts in this anthology:

Peter Scupham — 'The Nondescript' from *The Snowing Globe* © Peter Scupham 1972, reprinted by permission of Peterloo Poets; 'Prehistories' and 'Wind and Absence' from *Prehistories* © Oxford University Press 1975; 'Effacements', 'Marginalia', 'The Doves', 'Trencrom' and 'Atlantic' from *The Hinterland* © Oxford University Press 1977; 'The Chain' and 'The Beach' from *Summer Palaces* © Peter Scupham 1980, all reprinted by permission of Oxford University Press, 'The Ornamental Hermits' from *Transformation Scenes* and 'Madelon', the first part of 'Notes from a War Diary' © Peter Scupham 1983, reprinted by permission of the author and published in *Winter Quarters* by Oxford University Press.

Tony Harrison — 'Thomas Campey and the Copernican System' and 'The Nuptial Torches' from *The Loiners* published by London Magazine Editions; 'On Not Being Milton', 'Classics Society', 'National Trust' and 'Book Ends' from *The School of Eloquence*; 'Continuous' and 'Art and Extinction' from *Continuous* published by Rex Collings Ltd.; 'A Kumquat for John Keats' published by Bloodaxe Books Ltd., all © Tony Harrison 1968, 1978, 1981, 1982, 1983 and reprinted by permission of the author.

Gillian Clarke — 'Journey', 'Dyddgu Replies to Dafydd' and 'Waterfall' from *The Sundial* © Gillian Clarke 1978, published by Gomer Press and reprinted by permission of the author; other poems from *Letter from a Far Country* © Gillian Clarke 1982, and reprinted by permission of Carcanet Press Ltd.

Andrew Waterman — 'The Song' and 'The Two Roads' © Andrew Waterman 1974, from *Living Room*, published by Marvell Press and reprinted by permission of the author; 'A Winter's Tale' (uncollected) printed by permission of the author © Andrew Waterman 1983; other poems from *From the Other Country, Over the Wall* and *Out for the Elements* © Andrew Waterman 1977, 1980, 1983, reprinted by permission of Carcanet Press Ltd.

Derek Mahon — 'The Forger', 'An Image from Beckett', 'Consolations of Philosophy', 'Dog Days', 'The Snow Party', 'A Disused Shed in Co. Wexford' and 'The Return' © Derek Mahon 1979, from *Poems 1962-1978*; 'Courtyards in Delft', 'North Wind, Portrush', 'The Andean Flute', 'Tractatus' and 'The Woods' from *The Hunt by Night* © Derek Mahon 1982, all reprinted by permission of Oxford University Press.